Figures

COMPOUND RISK ANALYSIS OF NATURAL HAZARDS AND INFECTIOUS DISEASE OUTBREAKS

APRIL 2022

© 2022 Asian Development Bank
6 ADB Avenue, Mandaluyong City, 1550 Metro Manila, Philippines
Tel +63 2 8632 4444; Fax +63 2 8636 2444
www.adb.org

Some rights reserved. Published in 2022.

ISBN 978-92-9269-450-0 (print); 978-92-9269-451-7 (electronic); 978-92-9269-452-4 (ebook)
Publication Stock No. TCS220131-2
DOI: http://dx.doi.org/10.22617/TCS220131-2

Note:
In this publication, "$" refers to United States dollars.

Cover design by Francis Manio.

On the cover: Natural hazards and infectious disease outbreaks. When occurring as compound events, these can add significant pressure on countries' socioeconomic and physical vulnerabilities and require accurate and effective investment in risk management.

Contents

Tables and Figures

Acknowledgments

This study was undertaken on behalf of the Central Asia Regional Economic Cooperation (CAREC) Secretariat and the Asian Development Bank under the technical assistance, Developing a Disaster Risk Transfer Facility in the CAREC Region. The team would like to thank Junkyu Lee, director, Chief Financial Sector Group, Sustainable Development and Climate Change Department; Safdar Parvez, advisor, Office of the Director General, East Asia Department; Thomas Kessler, principal finance specialist (Disaster Insurance), Sustainable Development and Climate Change Department; Carmen Garcia Perez, regional cooperation specialist, Regional Cooperation and Operations Coordination Division, Central and West Asia Department; Irene de Roma, programs officer, Central and West Asia Department; and Jennifer Lapis, CAREC regional cooperation coordinator, for the overall support and guidance.

The team also expresses its appreciation to the regional cooperation coordinators and national focal points advisors in all CAREC member countries for their assistance in organizing and hosting virtual consultations. The team would also like to extend its gratitude to senior officials in CAREC member countries for their inputs, feedback, and contributions.

The authors of this study were Christopher Au, Simon Young, and David Simmons at Willis Towers Watson; and Ben Oppenheim, Nita Madhav, Nicole Stephenson, and Jaclyn Guerrero at Metabiota. Data contributions have been provided by the Global Earthquake Model Foundation and JBA Risk Management.

Abbreviations

ADB	Asian Development Bank
CAREC	Central Asia Regional Economic Cooperation
CFR	case fatality rate
COVID-19	coronavirus disease
IMAR	Inner Mongolia Autonomous Region
MMI	modified Mercalli intensity
PRC	People's Republic of China
UN	United Nations
WASH	water, sanitation, and hygiene
WHO	World Health Organization
XUAR	Xinjiang Uygur Autonomous Region

Executive Summary

The multiyear nature of the coronavirus disease (COVID-19) pandemic provides the conditions for a compound event. The likelihood of a natural hazard occurring in a country affected by COVID-19 is high. This compound risk scenario is not theoretical, but one which has played out across the member countries of the Central Asia Regional Economic Cooperation (CAREC). Flooding in Afghanistan in May 2020, in the Kyrgyz Republic in May 2020, and in Georgia in August 2020 are some examples. Similarly, a 5.9 magnitude earthquake in February 2021 affected Pakistan and Tajikistan. CAREC member countries will continue to face compound risk, not just for the duration of the COVID-19 pandemic, but on an ongoing basis, as various types of natural hazards potentially co-occur and compound each other.

Compound risk occurs when two or more shock events overlap, inducing additional pressure on social and physical vulnerability and/or initiating a chain of further stressors. In theory, the impact of a compound event are potentially much higher than those of two events occurring discretely. Damage to physical and social infrastructure and existing emergency needs occupy the bandwidth of government, civil society, households, and businesses. Additional pressure from a new shock may deepen existing vulnerabilities and undermine response efforts.

The compound risk between a natural hazard event and an infectious disease outbreak may occur in various ways. A natural hazard during an infectious disease outbreak is one form of compound risk. A second is an infectious disease outbreak trigerred by a natural hazard. Damaged health infrastructure, increased standing water and ruptured sewage systems, mass relocation of populations, and emergency response efforts can all increase the risk of an infectious disease outbreak. These are direct causation factors occuring in this second form of compound risk.

However, empirical evidence suggests natural hazard events generally do not trigger serious epidemics. Though there are a number of mechanisms which could amplify such risk, these do not appear material to sparking a sizeable outbreak. The vast majority of flood and earthquake events are not followed by subsequent outbreaks. Where these are observed, such as following repeated flooding in Pakistan, the outbreaks tend to be localized and eliminated quickly. That many disaster events do not trigger outbreaks is partially attributed to disaster risk management measures, particularly through the substantial communication and warning efforts of the World Health Organization, United Nations agencies, and other humanitarian response actors. For example, in response to extreme flooding along the Indus River in 2010, the Pakistan Ministry of Health and World Health Organization expanded the existing disease early warning system to support outbreak detection and management in flood-affected provinces. While further improvements were made following the event, the early warning system is thought to have contributed positively to reducing flood-related outbreaks.

The recent experience of the COVID-19 pandemic has shown the impacts a natural hazard can bring during an outbreak. It was likely that countries would experience natural hazard events while responding to COVID-19. Despite expectation in academe and media for an intensification to the pattern of infections and deaths, the recorded impact of a natural hazard during the pandemic was muted. Some locations saw a measurable increase in COVID-19 spread and mortality, though these were not significant enough to stand out in the yearly trajectory. For example, detailed studies showed that the wide-ranging impacts of Hurricane Iota on the Colombian island archipelago of San Andrés, Providencia, and Santa Catalina did not lead to a corresponding spike in COVID-19 infections. The same is true in Mexico and Louisiana, when faced with powerful tropical cyclones during the 2020 Atlantic hurricane season.

Representative earthquake and flood events impacting assets, populations, and critical healthcare infrastructure were modeled and incorporated into simulations of pandemic events. A 1-in-200-year event footprint, as representative of a severe event, was input into a Susceptible–Exposed–Infectious–Removed infectious disease modeling framework for pandemic influenza. Previous work for CAREC member countries identified pandemic influenza as the largest infectious disease risk. This modeling methodology reveals how the disruption and damage from a natural hazard may affect the ability of a country to manage their ongoing response to outbreak and disease spread.

The spatial extent of earthquake risk appears to be more influential than that of flooding, with a more significant impact on disease spread. Timing of the disaster event, relative to the phase of the pandemic influenza outbreak has an important impact on infectious disease outcomes.

However, the intensification of pandemic influenza impacts following a natural hazard is generally small. In some locations, there is a sizable uptick in infections and deaths; for example in Pakistan, these impacts have more than doubled. Yet, the events being modeled are extreme and rare. The modeled flood and earthquake events are 1-in-200-year and the influenza pandemic is likewise between a 1-in-100- and 1-in-200-year event. For reference, Metabiota currently estimates that the COVID-19 pandemic is roughly a 0.25–0.33 annual exceedance probability, or a roughly 25–33-year event; these estimates should be interpreted with due caution, as the pandemic is not yet over, and losses continue to accumulate. These are tail risk events which induce large-scale impacts. The increase in influenza spread is moderate in this context.

Though the management approach for natural hazard differs from that of an infectious disease outbreak, these risks can usefully be seen as part of a continuum. Governments must address risk management in a multidisciplinary manner to account for the potential for compound risk. It appears in some locations such as Pakistan, appropriate management has helped reduce risk to tolerable levels. Preparing for compound risk is therefore possible. Moreover, government awareness of this potential risk can reinforce the case for continued investment in management measures that contribute to event response and ongoing risk management (e.g., outbreak preparedness to prevent an outbreak from crossing a threshold). When compound risk is taken into account, investment in risk management becomes more accurate and effective.

1 Introduction

1.1 Overview

The recent coronavirus disease (COVID-19) pandemic has exposed the compounding nature of extreme risk. The increased vulnerability of individuals, communities, countries, and regions induced by the management response and associated negative economic consequences have been evident. The multiyear nature of COVID-19 means a variety of natural hazard events have occurred while societies were already subject to transmission management measures and consequential economic vulnerability, as well as health system overload.

Compound risk occurs when two or more shock events overlap, inducing additional pressure on social and physical vulnerability and/or initiating a chain of further stressors. An amplification of risk factors is expected from a compound risk event, potentially deepening existing vulnerabilities. The extent of these impacts is typically beyond a single jurisidiction, with regional implications. The anticipated impact of a compound event is in excess of events occurring individually. Therefore, understanding compound risk is essential to avoid underestimating potential losses and underappreciating system dynamics.[1]

Compound risk is multifaceted and manifests through different mechanisms. The occurrence of a natural hazard during an infectious disease outbreak is one type. Another type is the triggering of an infectious disease outbreak following a flood, earthquake, or other natural hazards. Damage to health infrastructure, increased standing water and ruptured sewage systems, mass relocation of populations, and emergency response efforts can all increase the risk of an outbreak.

This study covers two transmission chains: (i) a natural hazard event during a pandemic, and (ii) a natural hazard triggering or being quickly followed by an outbreak of an infectious disease. The theoretical mechanisms for compounding and evidence base of recorded impacts globally are reviewed for both forms of compound risk. Deterministic scenarios of a natural hazard occurring during an outbreak are developed for member countries of the Central Asia Regional Economic Cooperation (CAREC) program.[2] Though much historical work concentrates on outbreaks following major disaster events, such events have been rare, and are not well-captured in the modeling environment.

Compounding of natural hazard perils is always possible and the broad consequences of such compounding can be predicted. For instance, an earthquake affecting a region that has just had a major flood event is likely to have a greater impact than when the flooding had not occurred. This can be traditionally captured through allowing for the random co-occurrence of uncorrelated events. For infectious disease risk, the calculus is different. Epidemics and pandemics are generally long-lasting events; they are bigger stressors on disaster preparedness and

---

[1] I. Monasterolo, M. Billio, and S. Battiston. 2020. *The Importance of Compound Risk in the Nexus of COVID-19, Climate Change and Finance. Working Paper.* Venice: Ca' Foscari University of Venice, Department of Economics.

[2] CAREC member countries are Afghanistan, Azerbaijan, Georgia, Kazakhstan, the Kyrgyz Republic, Mongolia, Pakistan, the People's Republic of China (Inner Mongolia Autonomous Region and Xinjiang Uygur Autonomous Region), Tajikistan, Turkmenistan, and Uzbekistan. The Asian Development Bank (ADB) placed on hold its assistance in Afghanistan effective 15 August 2021. All references to Afghanistan in this report are based on information available as of 30 July 2021.

response system (including the health system), and their evolution in a particular country can be highly nonlinear (such that even a modest additional stressor can radically increase disease transmission and its impacts on population health).

This study is part of a technical assistance that aims to strengthen disaster risk management and financing in the CAREC region. Earthquake, flood, and infectious disease outbreak risk have been modeled. Analysis of COVID-19 case histories, transmission mitigation measures, and potential COVID-19 outcome scenarios were presented to member governments. This study advances such work, to understand the potential impacts of compounding risk between natural hazards and infectious disease outbreaks. The objective is to provide an indication of the materiality of this risk and advice for future management so that governments can prepare and make informed decisions regarding disaster risk financing.

1.2 Report Structure

This report profiles the potential outcomes of natural hazard risk and infectious disease outbreak compound events.

Section 2 introduces theoretical mechanisms for compounding in both directions, and presents global and regional case studies. Section 3 provides the results of modeling to profile potential outcomes of a severe flood or earthquake occurring during an outbreak in CAREC member countries. Section 4 concludes with considerations for future disaster risk management.

2 Mechanisms for Compound Risk

This section illustrates the theoretical mechanisms by which risk is amplified through compound events. As identified in Section 1, compound risk between a natural hazard event and an infectious disease outbreak can work in two broad ways: (i) a natural hazard event occurring during an outbreak, or (ii) a natural hazard event triggering an outbreak.

These two concepts are centered on understanding how physical and social vulnerability are affected following these events. The mechanisms and pathways by which risk may be amplified in each of these scenarios are now identified and explored.

2.1 Natural Hazard Event During an Outbreak

The COVID-19 pandemic demonstrates the extent to which social vulnerability is exacerbated during an outbreak. Transmission reduction measures implemented during an outbreak, such as social distancing, and impacts of the outbreak, such as increased sick staff, would be expected to amplify the vulnerability to a natural hazard event. All things considered, it is logical to assume that the impacts of a natural hazard would be increased during an outbreak, compared to a baseline scenario of no outbreak.

The primary mechanisms by which risk is amplified include the following:

(i) **Higher physical damage due to reduced implementation and effectiveness of preparedness measures.** Disaster management and emergency agency capacity tends to be limited. When faced with overlapping events, the full range of services are unlikely to be delivered, spanning immediate response and longer term recovery. In the short term, early warning systems and emergency mitigation measures may not be implemented with the same efficiency and extent, for example, due to decreased staff availability or restrictions on activities. More broadly, funds may have already been diverted toward outbreak response, depleting the available funds and requiring additional procedures, hence delaying the response effort.

(ii) **Higher human impact due to a less resilient population.** An infectious disease outbreak imposes material strain on populations and health systems. Excess capacity in a health system is often nonexistent during an outbreak. Compared to no outbreak, the health system during an outbreak is less able to treat citizens affected by the natural hazard event due to diminishing medical resources. Additional concerns on the behavioral response from citizens at risk, such as willingness to evacuate and using public shelters and common food and water sources, are also relevant.

(iii) **Higher economic impact due to a slower recovery.** An implication of the above drivers is slowing the speed of recovery from the natural hazard event relative to the "normal" case. Household, corporate, and sovereign finances are likely to be negatively affected during an outbreak. The additional impact of a natural hazard will require futher financial support from the government and/or from international aid. The speed of response and financial support to restore physical and human capital is well correlated with reducing the overall economic impact of the natural hazard event.[3]

---

[3] S. Hallegatte. 2015. The Indirect Cost of Natural Disasters and an Economic Definition of Macroeconomic Resilience. *Policy Research Working Paper.* No. 7357. Washington, DC: World Bank Group.

The collective outcome of these three mechanisms is to increase the vulnerability of a country and its population to the natural hazard event. It is reasonable to expect a worse performance when compared to a scenario of no outbreak. Put another way, the existing natural hazard resilience of a country and relevant infrastructure is diminished due to outbreak response.

Further, some form of feedback is to be expected. A natural hazard may affect disease spread itself, changing the dynamics of the outbreak. Outbreak response measures may be impacted by the natural hazard. The dynamics of this compound risk are complex. Section 3 discusses the modeling of such interaction.

2.2 Natural Hazard Event Triggering an Outbreak

Damage and impacts from a natural hazard event may create the conditions for an infectious disease outbreak. This is another mechanism by which these risks may compound. Damage to healthcare facilities, evacuation of people, and the presence of standing water and/or rupturing of sewage infrastructure all increase the physical vulnerability of an area to some types of infectious disease outbreaks. The emergency response and recovery effort introduces new personnel and materials. Taken together, the necessary conditions to trigger an outbreak may exist or be exacerbated in the aftermath of a disaster event.

Risk drivers can be categorized across three mechanisms:

(i) **Reduced ability to respond to an outbreak.** In parallel with the first form of compound risk, a natural hazard may temporarily impair outbreak preparedness, with hospitals damaged or closed, key staff unavailable, medicines and their distribution limited, and disaster response agencies under pressure. Early cases of an outbreak may pass undetected or with insufficient organizational bandwidth to respond appropriately.

(ii) **Increased likely spread due to displacement/migration and close proximity of displaced people.** The displacement of population following a natural hazard into evacuation centers in the short term and temporary camps in the medium term increases the vulnerability of the population to an outbreak. Water, sanitation, and hygiene (WASH) infrastructure may be hastily arranged or inadequate for the total volume and intensity of use. Water supply can quickly become contaminated.

(iii) **Disrupted supply of essential resources.** A large natural hazard is likely to induce disruption to the supply of food and clean water. The opportunity for disease spread increases under these conditions.

A review of 132 post-disaster outbreaks reveals the most common risk factors and how they vary across different forms of disaster events. Each type of disaster event is represented by a color, with the total number of events listed in the legend. The height of the bar, showing the proportion of the main risk factors in infectious disease outbreaks, reveals the frequency of the risk factor identified across different disaster event classifications.

Population displacement is the most frequently reported risk factor, with WASH risk factors second, as shown in Figure 1. In practice these factors often go hand-in-hand. In situations of significant population displacement, living conditions can deteriorate dramatically, increasing the risk of disease due to inadequate sanitation and lack of access to clean water.

Diseases that are most likely to follow a natural hazard can be classified into three categories: (i) waterborne diseases such as those causing diarrheal symptoms, Hepatitis A and Hepatitis E, and Leptospirosis; (ii) diseases associated with crowding including measles, meningitis, and acute respiratory infections; and (iii) vector-borne diseases including malaria and dengue.

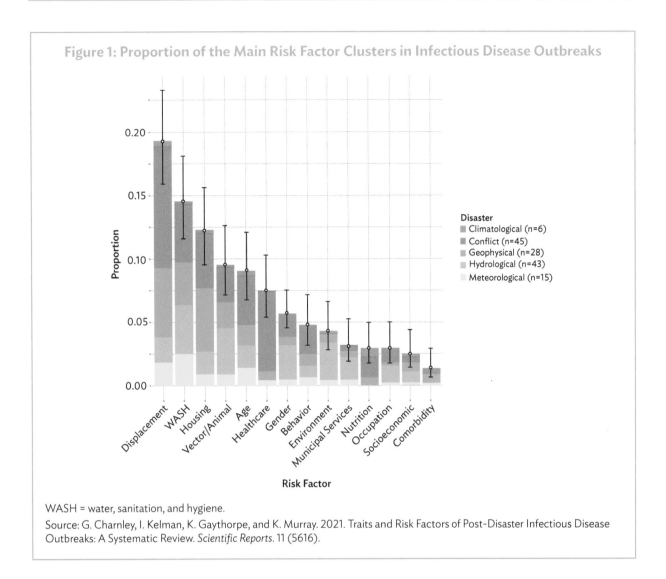

Figure 1: Proportion of the Main Risk Factor Clusters in Infectious Disease Outbreaks

WASH = water, sanitation, and hygiene.
Source: G. Charnley, I. Kelman, K. Gaythorpe, and K. Murray. 2021. Traits and Risk Factors of Post-Disaster Infectious Disease Outbreaks: A Systematic Review. *Scientific Reports*. 11 (5616).

Other types of human-induced hazards may create similar potential for risk amplification, via similar causal channels. Armed conflict is a notable example. Armed conflict has direct, destructive effects on health and sanitation infrastructure. It can erode state capacity to respond to outbreaks and deliver health services by, among other factors, constraining access to affected geographies. Armed conflict can also induce population displacement which may increase population vulnerability.[4] These dynamics contributed to the long duration and severity of the North Kivu ebolavirus epidemic,[5] and have posed similar challenges to COVID-19 response in conflict-affected settings.

2.3 Case Studies of Compound Events

The illustrated theoretical mechanisms for risk amplification are now compared against notable events of compounding disaster risk and infectious disease outbreaks. Case studies based on research of both formats of compound risk are described in pages 6–9. The scientific literature on compound risk is still in its early phases,

---

[4]   M. Gayer, D. Legros, P. Formenty, and M. Connolly. 2007. Conflict and Emerging Infectious Diseases. *Emerging Infectious Diseases*. 13 (11): 1625.
[5]   O. Kalenga, M. Moeti, A. Sparrow, V. Nguyen, D. Lucey, and T. Ghebreyesus. 2019. The Ongoing Ebola Epidemic in the Democratic Republic of Congo, 2018–2019. *New England Journal of Medicine*. 381 (4). pp. 373–383.

and data, as well as robust analyses, of risk compounding effects are relatively limited. The existing historical analyses primarily capture easily measurable aspects of a compound event, such as earthquake intensity or cyclone windspeed, rather than the complex, intersecting socioeconomic effects.

Natural Hazard During an Outbreak

The COVID-19 pandemic has increased attention on the impact of natural hazard events on existing disease outbreaks. In anticipation of floods, earthquakes, and tropical cyclones, in various locations, modeling was conducted to anticipate the potential impact of these natural hazards on COVID-19 spread. Likewise, following the occurrence of events, studies were carried out to investigate the experienced impact.

The broad trend is of a large differential between predicted impact and actual experience. In several examples, recorded COVID-19 infections and deaths did not increase materially following the onset of a natural hazard event. Isolating the impact of the event is often difficult, given the number of factors that can coexist (e.g., availability of testing, changing control measures). Moreover, anticipatory modeling of potential impacts and management measures could have been effective in triggering preemptive action, reducing disease spread.

Countries at different stages of development and epidemic preparedness exhibited a zero material increase in transmission. There are competing claims as to why this might be the case, including the concern on compound risk and the associated narrative that may have heightened government awareness, commitment, and preparedness to natural hazard risk. This may have been true of households and businesses too. It is thus possible that the prospect of compound risk has helped reduce the overall economic impact by improving response. A series of case studies on large-scale events around the world are presented to illustrate this further. Cases were selected for study based on the large-scale nature of the natural hazard event, the quality of data for evaluation, and dedicated, existing research.

Earthquake, Croatia, 2020. A 5.4 magnitude earthquake struck north of Zagreb in March 2020, as the COVID-19 crisis was unfolding across Europe.[6] Despite much concern on the potential of an earthquake and its aftershocks to accelerate disease transmission, there was no detectable increase in the incidence of COVID-19.[7] Another earthquake occurred in December 2020, with the same result on COVID-19 spread. The March 2020 earthquake appeared particularly potent, with the extent of COVID-19 spread across Europe increasingly visible at that time. However, neither government response nor economic loss (dominantly composed of damaged or destroyed building stock) appear to have been measurably affected by the COVID-19 pandemic. Indeed, it is arguable that identification of the potential for increased impacts due to COVID-19 motivated a more robust response from the European Commission[8] and a broader crisis response from the international community than what might otherwise have been the case.

Hurricane Laura, United States, 2020 is a Category 4 hurricane that impacted the Caribbean and the Gulf coast, midwestern, and eastern United States on 20–29 August 2020. An investigative modeling study on four counties in southeast Florida simulated the impact of increased transmission resulting from pre-evacuation and evacuation activities the month before the arrival of Hurricane Laura.[9] Depending on the chosen transmissibility scenario, this modeling predicted a mean increase in case numbers of 2.6%–8.3% from the "origin" counties (those from which people are

6   J. Atalić, M. Uroš, M. Šavor Novak, M. Demšić, and M. Nastev. 2021. The Mw5.4 Zagreb (Croatia) Earthquake of March 22, 2020: Impacts and Response. *Bulletin of Earthquake Engineering*. 19. pp. 3461–3489.

7   Rok Čivljak, Alemka Markotić, and Krunoslav Capak. 2020. Earthquake in the Time of COVID-19: The Story from Croatia (CroVID-20). *Journal of Global Health*. 10 (1). June.

8   It is notable that the Zagreb event occurred during the Croatian Presidency of the Council of the European Union, a clash of unlikely events with a likely positive net outcome.

9   S. Pei, K. Dahl, T. Yamana, R. Licker, and J Shaman. 2020. Compound Risks of Hurricane Evacuation Amid the Covid-19 Pandemic in the United States. *Geohealth*. 4 (12).

evacuated from), and a mean increase in cases of 0.38%–10.0% in "destination" counties (where people are evacuated to). By comparison, observational data from *The New York Times* over the same period showed a mean decrease in cases of 76% across the modeled counties. Cases continued to fall in the month following Hurricane Laura's landfall in Florida.

Hurricane Iota, Colombia, 2020 is a Category 5 hurricane that devastated the island of Providencia on 16 November 2020, causing extensive damage. Out of 337 people in shelters in Providencia, as of 28 November, there were 21 positive COVID-19 test results. Sixteen of these positive test results belonged to one shelter of 21 people, potentially indicating a spread of the virus in that shelter. Out of 84 people in shelters in San Andrés, one person tested positive for COVID-19. The archipelagoes of Colombia were less affected by the pandemic than mainland Colombia, which may have contributed to the low spread post-hurricane: only 82 total cases had been reported in Providencia as of 30 November, and 2,056 in San Andrés.[10] Weekly COVID-19 case numbers across San Andrés, Providencia, and Santa Catalina as at 14 December 2020, that is, the weeks following the passage of Hurricane Iota, did not significantly increase (Figure 2).[11] There is a small spike on the week of 22 November but this may be due to increased precautionary testing at shelters and is not definitive.

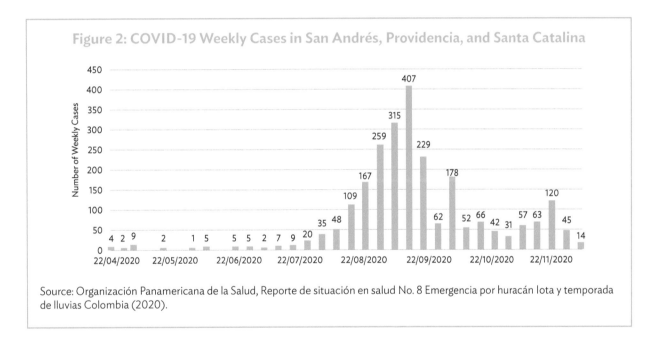

Figure 2: COVID-19 Weekly Cases in San Andrés, Providencia, and Santa Catalina

Source: Organización Panamericana de la Salud, Reporte de situación en salud No. 8 Emergencia por huracán Iota y temporada de lluvias Colombia (2020).

Tropical Storm Cristobal, Mexico, 2020. A study attempted to isolate the impact of Tropical Storm Cristobal on COVID-19 cases in the Yucatan Peninsula in Mexico and found no evidence of a direct link.[12] In the aftermath of the storm and heavy rainfall, 13 shelters were opened to 719 people. Although municipalities did see an increase in COVID-19 cases, this increase did not differ from the trend observed in the days prior to the event. The municipalities did implement specific protocols to prevent COVID-19 spread during this time and this may have contributed to the avoidance of significant outbreaks. Only one municipality showed a marked increase in cases, recording 44 cases compared to 10, one week prior to the event.

10   Organización Panamericana de la Salud (OPS). 2020. *Emergencia por huracán Iota y temporada de lluvias Colombia*. Reporte de situación en salud No. 8.
11   OPS. 2020. *Emergencia por huracán Iota y temporada de lluvias Colombia*. Reporte de situación en salud No. 11.
12   O. Frausto-Martinez, C. Aguilar-Becerra, O. Colin-Olivares, G. Sanchez-Rivera, A. Hafsi, A. Contreras-Tax, and W. Uhu-Yam. 2020. COVID-19, Storms and Floods: Impacts of Tropical Storm Cristobal in the Western Sector of the Yucatan Peninsula, Mexico. *Sustainability*. 12 (23): 9925.

Natural Hazard Triggering an Outbreak

There is a longer history of recorded outbreaks following the onset of disaster events. The evidence base again indicates reasonably low levels of compounding risk. Importantly, there is robust evidence suggesting that proactive management, centered on WASH factors, helps alleviate the risk of an outbreak.

Recurrent flooding, Bangladesh. Bangladesh registered numerous diarrhea and cholera outbreaks after floods in the 1980s, 1990s, and early 2000s. Following the floods in 2004, there was a diarrhea disease outbreak of 17,000 registered cases. In the 1988 floods, diarrhea disease was responsible for 27% of 154 flood-related deaths in rural Bangladesh.[13] *Vibrio cholerae* was the primary pathogen responsible for these diarrheal outbreaks in Dhaka.

Since then, Bangladesh has improved its flood preparation, providing water purification tablets and using bleach at shelters. The population is more conscious of preventive measures such as washing hands and buying bottled water. Doctors no longer report higher cases following a flood.[14] Through efficient post-disaster sanitation measures, Bangladesh is now able to successfully mitigate the risk of diarrheal outbreaks.

Flooding, Pakistan, 2010. Monsoon-driven flooding of the Indus River basin in 2010 impacted approximately 20 million people across the Balochistan, Khyber Pakhtunkhwa, Punjab, and Sindh regions resulting in just under 2,000 deaths.[15] The potential for infectious disease outbreaks following severe flooding was well recognized.[16] This has prompted Pakistan's Ministry of Health and the World Health Organization (WHO) to expand and enhance an existing disease early warning system.[17] Despite early fears of cholera cases numbering hundreds of thousands,[18] 5 months after the onset of flooding, 155 suspected cholera cases had been reported, just under half of which were confirmed through lab testing. Key enhancements to the existing system included standardized case definitions, establishing mobile clinics, training healthcare professionals, and publication of daily bulletins. While further improvements were made following the event, it is thought that the early actions contributed positively to reducing flood-related outbreaks, probably by several orders of magnitude.

Earthquake, Pakistan, 2005. A 7.6 magnitude earthquake brought an estimated death toll of 87,350 in Pakistan.[19] Approximately 2.8 million people were displaced in Pakistan. Various infectious disease outbreaks were observed in the aftermath. This included an acute watery diarrhea outbreak in northern Pakistan in an unplanned and poorly equipped camp of 2,000 people with no running water or sewage pipes.[20] There were also 1,200 cases of acute jaundice reported, many confirmed as hepatitis E and a few hundred sporadic cases of measles, mostly in communities in crowded shelters with low vaccination rates. After the 2008 earthquake, there were also cases of fever, respiratory infections, acute diarrhea, acute jaundice, and scabies.

13   B. Schwartz et al. 2006. Diarrheal Epidemics in Dhaka, Bangladesh, During Three Consecutive Floods: 1988, 1998, and 2004. *The American Journal of Tropical Medicine and Hygiene.* Vol. 74 (6). pp. 1067–73.

14   K. Chowdhury. 2017. Bangladesh Eliminates Post-Flood Disease Deaths. *The Third Pole.* 30 August. https://www.thethirdpole.net/en/livelihoods/bangladesh-eliminates-post-flood-disease-deaths/.

15   Singapore Red Cross. 2010. Pakistan Floods: The Deluge of Disaster – Facts & Figures as of 15 September 2010. https://reliefweb.int/report/pakistan/pakistan-floodsthe-deluge-disaster-facts-figures-15-september-2010.

16   M. Baqir et al. 2012. Infectious Diseases in the Aftermath of Monsoon Flooding in Pakistan. *Asian Pac J Trop Biomed.* January. 2 (1). pp. 76–79. doi: 10.1016/S2221-1691(11)60194-9. PMID: 23569839; PMCID: PMC3609207.

17   Centers for Disease Control and Prevention (CDC). 2012. Early Warning Disease Surveillance After a Flood Emergency—Pakistan, 2010. *Morbidity and Mortality Weekly Report.* https://www.cdc.gov/mmwr/preview/mmwrhtml/mm6149a2.htm.

18   CNN. 2010. Officials Fear Disease Outbreak in Flood-Hit Pakistan. http://edition.cnn.com/2010/WORLD/asiapcf/08/02/pakistan.flooding/index.html.

19   Earthquake Engineering Research Institute. 2006. The Kashmir Earthquake of October 8, 2005: Impacts in Pakistan. https://reliefweb.int/report/pakistan/kashmir-earthquake-october-8-2005-impacts-pakistan#:~:text=The%20Pakistani%20government%E2%80%99s%20official%20death,over%203.5%20million%20rendered%20homeless.

20   The New Humanitarian. 2005. Pakistan: More than 400 Cases of Watery Diarrhoea in Quake Camp. https://reliefweb.int/report/pakistan/pakistan-more-400-cases-watery-diarrhoea-quake-camp.

Tsunami, Indian Ocean, 2004. Despite reports immediately after the tsunami quoting significant risk of infectious disease and vector abundance, there were no measurable increases in cases of malaria or dengue fever. Strict preventive measures were put in place in camps, including clean water and organization of the displaced into small, rather than large camps; and there were no cholera outbreaks. As expected from a tsunami, there were many cases of aspiration pneumonia. Many cases of aspiration pneumonia, as well as community-acquired pneumonia, were also observed after the 2011 Japan tsunami.

Earthquake, Haiti, 2010. A catastrophic 7.0 magnitude earthquake struck Haiti on 12 January 2010. More than a quarter of a million people were estimated to have died as a result of the earthquake, with at least 300,000 injured, and 5 million, half of the population, displaced. The earthquake severely damaged the already weak infrastructure and public sanitation systems, creating conditions that could greatly facilitate the spread of infectious diseases. Nine months after the earthquake, on 20 October 2010, Haiti's first ever cholera outbreak was confirmed. This outbreak grew into the world's most severe cholera epidemic in recent history.[21] The epidemic lasted most of the decade until the last case was confirmed in January 2019. Through the course of the epidemic, 820,000 cholera cases were diagnosed with nearly 10,000 deaths.[22]

Cholera arrived in Haiti just days after a new contingent of peacekeepers joined the United Nations Stabilization Mission in Haiti. The Nepalese peacekeepers had come from a country in which an identical strain of the disease was prevalent. While many initially argued that the outbreak began when the nonpathogenic *Vibrio cholerae* found in the coastal waters of Haiti was given the right environmental conditions to evolve into a pathogenic strain, scientific evidence points overwhelmingly to the conclusion that the arrival of Nepalese peacekeepers and the start of the outbreak are linked with one another.[23]

The UN Secretary-General established a panel of independent experts in January 2011 to examine the source of the epidemic. The panel also rejected the theory that the outbreak began through environmental disruption and further that the introduction of cholera by peacekeepers was not, in itself, solely responsible for the epidemic; rather, the panel suggested that the underdevelopment coupled with ideal environmental and epidemiological conditions from the catastrophic earthquake, including widespread disruption of water and sanitation systems, caused the disaster to unfold and reach such severe levels of disease transmission.[24]

Considerations

Case studies of natural hazards occurring during an outbreak are based on quantitative evidence documented in 2020. In all instances, recorded COVID-19 infections and deaths were not significantly different following the natural hazard event. Part of this may be due to the timing of the outbreak. For example, in San Andrés, Providencia, and Santa Catalina, case numbers were falling, several weeks after the peak, and so the baseload of cases was low. If a natural hazard event occurs when a country is experiencing rapidly mounting disease spread, then the impact may be more significant.

Similarly, case studies detailing natural hazards triggering an outbreak reveal that though the background conditions for outbreaks exist following a natural hazard, these rarely spark into major events. There are many documented cases of outbreaks following natural hazards, but most of these events are small in significance, with low case numbers and localized clusters. The exceptions, such as the case of cholera in Haiti, occur primarily in low-income

21 Centers for Disease Control and Prevention. Cholera in Haiti. https://www.cdc.gov/cholera/haiti/index.html.
22 Ministere Sante Publique et de la Population. 2020. Rapport du Réseau National de Surveillance: Choléra. Haiti. https://mspp.gouv.ht/site/downloads/Profil%20statistique%20Cholera%203eme%20SE%202020.pdf.
23 R. Frerichs et al. 2012. Nepalese Origin of Cholera Epidemic in Haiti. *Clinical Microbiology and Infection.* 18 (6). pp. E158–E163; R. Piarroux et al. 2011. Understanding the Cholera Epidemic, Haiti. *Emerging Infectious Diseases.* 17 (7): 1161.
24 United Nations General Assembly. 2016. Report of the Special Rapporteur on Extreme Poverty and Human Rights. https://reliefweb.int/sites/reliefweb.int/files/resources/N1627119.pdf.

or conflict-affected countries where infrastructure, disease control systems, and health systems more broadly are either fragile or under greater stress, and therefore may be less capable of mitigating potential upticks in disease transmission following an exogenous shock.

The global spread and persistence of COVID-19 means that the notable influx of external institutions and people that accompany post-disaster humanitarian response and reconstruction activities presents the risk of importing disease which could spark local infections. This is especially true in fragile countries which may not be well-equipped to screen and manage a sudden influx of potentially infected people, particularly when the focus is on natural hazard event response.

Health officials and the media often talk of the risk of post-disaster infectious disease. However, a series of measures, centered on WASH, appear to be highly effective in containing potential outbreaks, and in many cases external humanitarian assistance flows are substantial and may play an important role in containing potential secondary impacts. As noted, the earthquake in Haiti is an exception, but demonstrates the vigilance required as part of the emergency response effort.

Importantly, where there has not been large population displacement, the compound risk appears to be very low.[25] Outbreaks are less frequently reported in disaster-affected populations than in conflict-affected populations, where communicable disease is a major cause of death.[26]

---

[25]   I. Kouadio, S. Aljunid, T. Kamigaki, K. Hammad, and H. Oshitani. 2012. Infectious Diseases Following Natural Disasters: Prevention and Control Measures. *Expert Review of Anti-Infective Therapy*. 10 (1). pp. 95–104.

[26]   A. Culver, R. Rochat, and S. Cookson. 2017. Public Health Implications of Complex Emergencies and Natural Disasters. *Conflict and Health*. 11 (32).

3 Compound Scenarios

3.1 Overview

This section presents the results of several modeled disaster compound scenarios showing the progression of a pandemic combined with the impact of a natural hazard.[27] These scenarios explore the impact of an earthquake and a flood on an influenza pandemic.

The analysis quantifies the impact of representative earthquake and flood events on built assets, populations, and critical healthcare infrastructure in each CAREC member country. These impacts are then used in a Susceptible–Exposed–Infectious–Removed infectious disease modeling framework. This simulates the consequences of a catastrophic flood or earthquake event for infectious disease spread, healthcare system response, and ability to bring closure to an outbreak.

These compound scenarios can be compared to a baseline scenario in which no other disaster event occurs. These results provide an understanding of the potential compounded effect of a disaster event during a pandemic. Such an occurrence is both impactful and scientifically plausible, particularly given the long duration of some pandemic events, and seasonal dynamics in some natural hazards such as flooding.

Models can be used to estimate the compounded effects at any frequency or severity level of interest. As described in section 3.2, this study has chosen to analyze compounded effects for roughly 1-in-200-year events. Focusing on the intersection of highly remote severe shocks might yield more dramatic illustrations of compounding effects, but would be of little practical analytic utility relative to exploring higher probability compounding dynamics which are more likely to confront policymakers. The probability of two randomly distributed 1-in-200-year events occurring in the same year is 1-in-40,000, which is well beyond the likelihood range traditionally considered for scenario events in a disaster planning context.

The modeling output primarily focuses on public health impacts rather than losses to national income. Economic loss modeling of compound risk is in its infancy. If any, there are only a few sophisticated economic models that capture, in an integrated fashion, the complex and sometimes contradictory effects that multiple hazards can introduce. In a hazard risk modeling context, for example, the economic losses introduced by flooding and an infectious disease outbreak would simply be summed. However, the true economic loss profile is likely to be far more complex. For example, if public health restrictions are relaxed to allow for immediate reconstruction and recovery from the flood, the impact of the outbreak on unemployment and in the aggregate might be mitigated, even if the overall total infection or mortality count increased. Likewise, remote working due to a pandemic could significantly mitigate injury and death because workers could be spared from a city-center earthquake occurring on a workday. Further study and model development is needed to more accurately capture these types of complex interacting effects.

---

[27] These scenarios are designed to help provide insight into the potential combined impact of a natural hazard during a pandemic under the specified assumptions. The results are generated using hazard risk and epidemiological models. All models are simplifications of real-world processes and cannot fully account for all factors involved in disease spread. The purpose of these scenarios is not to predict future compounded natural hazards and outbreaks, but to provide an illustrative example of the potential outcomes that could occur under the chosen assumptions. The actual event or outcome that occurs may differ substantially from these scenarios. Please exercise caution when using the results for decision-making purposes.

3.2 Methodology

The scenarios focus on areas of concentrated exposure within each CAREC member country (Table 1). Most of the selected locations are capital cities, to capture areas of the highest value at risk and major population centers. Alternative areas were selected in some places, to account for the nature of the hazard (e.g., Pakistan) or exposure (e.g., Kazakhstan). These areas are important as population density and distribution exert an influence on infections and deaths from a disease outbreak. Critical healthcare infrastructure, which may be damaged in a disaster event but are essential in responding to an outbreak, are also likely to be located in these areas.

Table 1: Areas of Concentrated Exposure

Location	Area of Concentrated Exposure
Afghanistan	Kabul
Azerbaijan	Baku
China, People's Republic of – Inner Mongolia Autonomous Region	Baotou
China, People's Republic of – Xinjiang Uygur Autonomous Region	Urumqi
Georgia	Tbilisi
Kazakhstan	Almaty
Kyrgyz Republic	Bishkek
Mongolia	Ulaanbaatar
Pakistan	Karachi for flood, Islamabad for earthquake
Tajikistan	Dushanbe
Turkmenistan	Ashgabat
Uzbekistan	Tashkent

Source: Asian Development Bank.

Natural Hazard Modeling

Natural hazard modeling was used to quantify the impact of representative 1-in-200-year earthquake and flood events across the CAREC member countries. Input return period hazard layers were derived from Jeremy Benn Associates' Global Flood Model and Global Earthquake Model's OpenQuake modeling platform. Two metrics of impact were modeled, and subsequently used as boundary conditions in the infectious disease modeling: (i) population affected, and (ii) damage rate to healthcare amenities, such as hospitals, clinics/doctors, laboratories, and pharmacies (Figure 3).

A 1-kilometer gridded population count dataset was used as basis for determining the population affected by 1-in-200-year earthquake and flood events.[28] For earthquake and flood events, hazard intensity was mapped to each population grid square. Then the hazard intensities were aggregated (into standard modified Mercalli intensity [MMI] scale units for earthquake, and 1-meter water depth intervals for flood), and the percentage population impacted by each intensity division was calculated (Table 2).

---

[28]   WorldPop. 2021. Unconstrained Individual Countries 2000–2020 UN Adjusted (1-kilometer resolution). https://www.worldpop.org/geodata/listing?id=75.

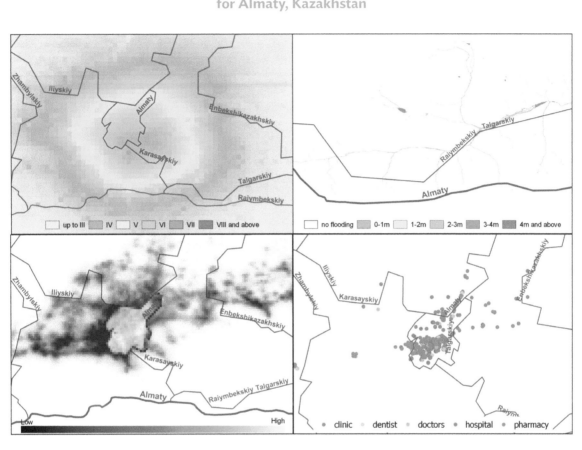

Figure 3: Natural Hazard and Exposure Inputs to Infectious Disease Clash Modeling for Almaty, Kazakhstan

Top from left to right Earthquake shaking map, Flood depth map (meters); *Bottom left to right* Population count, Healthcare facilities.
Sources: Global Earthquake Model; Jeremy Benn Associates; WorldPop; and healthsites.io.

Table 2: Population Affected by 1-in-200 Year Earthquake and Flood Events in Almaty, Kazakhstan

	Earthquake			Flood	
MMI Band	**Damage Description**	**Population Affected (%)**	**Flood Depth (m)**	**Damage Description**	**Population Affected (%)**
Up to III	None	28.43	None	None	99.57
IV	Light	10.71	Up to 1	Light	0.38
V	Moderate	12.43	1–2	Moderate	0.04
VI	Significant	35.95	2–3	Significant	0.00
VII	Severe	12.48	3–4	Severe	0.00
VIII and above	Complete	0.00	4 and above	Complete	0.01

m = meter, MMI = modified Mercalli intensity.
Source: Consultant team modeling.

A healthcare facilities dataset was used to quantify hazard impacts on different types of healthcare amenities.[29] The healthcare amenities included in this analysis were: (i) hospitals, which are critical for providing care to individuals who become seriously ill as a result of an infectious disease; (ii) clinics/doctors, who provide support to infected individuals; (iii) laboratories, which influence testing capacity and ability to detect novel variants; and (iv) pharmacies, which contribute to vaccine rollout. For earthquake and flood events, hazard intensity was mapped to each healthcare facility point. Then the hazard intensities were aggregated, and damage rates assigned to each hazard intensity. These damage rates were then aggregated to obtain a single damage rate for each healthcare facility (Table 3).

Table 3: Healthcare Amenity Damage Rate for 1-in-200-Year Earthquake Event in Almaty, Kazakhstan

Healthcare Amenity	Damage Rate (%)
Hospital	40.41
Clinic/Doctor	49.23
Laboratory	NA
Pharmacy	46.12

NA = data not available.
Source: Consultant team modeling.

Infectious Disease Modeling

The scenarios are generated using a deterministic, compartment model framework (Figure 4), which incorporates the epidemiological dynamics of pandemic influenza and the development of a prophylactic vaccine. Model parameterization is based on a review and analysis of epidemiological data and the latest scientific literature available.

To simulate disease spread, an epidemiologic model compartmentalizes human subpopulations by disease state. An individual can only exist in one disease state at any given time. The model probabilistically captures the progression of individuals through each disease state using a series of transition rate parameters that operate on a daily time step. The model utilizes a specialized compartmental structure specifically designed to capture the epidemiological dynamics of pandemic influenza, including vaccination. Transmission fluctuates seasonally with a peak in the winter and a trough in the summer consistent with what has been reported for historical pandemic influenza events.

Baseline Assumptions

The baseline assumptions and parameter values are selected to reflect a pandemic influenza event with a return period of approximately 100 to 200 years. Simulations are initiated with 100 initial infections and run for 3 years. The modeled scenarios include vaccination of the susceptible population starting at 9 months, accounting for development time of a vaccine for a novel pandemic influenza virus, which is applied for all CAREC member countries.

Once vaccination begins in the scenario, the susceptible population is vaccinated at a constant rate, which varies by epidemic preparedness until 65% of the population is vaccinated or until the simulation ends. The vaccine efficacy within the simulation is assumed to be 75%. The baseline reproduction number is 1.9 and decreases over time to 1.5 due to non-pharmaceutical interventions (e.g., social distancing). The case fatality ratio (CFR) varies by epidemic preparedness between 0.003 and 0.006.[30] The baseline parameter value assumptions are consistent with parameter values observed during prior influenza pandemics.

---

[29] Healthsites.io. 2021. https://healthsites.io/.
[30] Case fatality ratio refers to the number of deaths from the disease divided by the total number of cases of the disease.

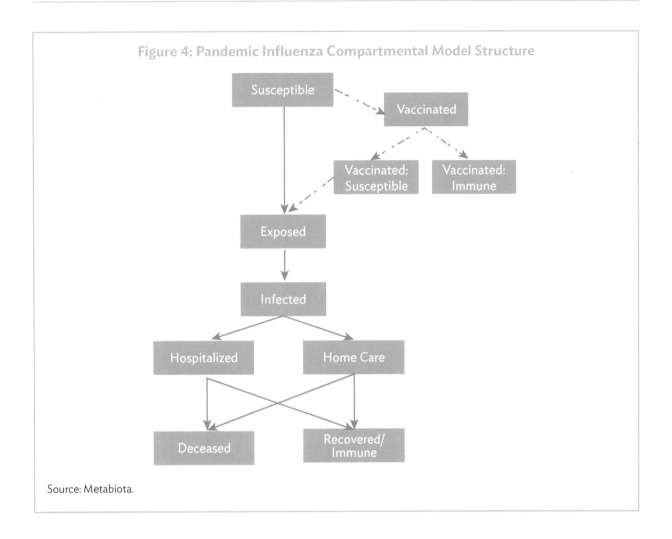

Figure 4: Pandemic Influenza Compartmental Model Structure

Source: Metabiota.

Earthquake Clash Scenario

The earthquake clash scenario is a combination of the influenza pandemic described above and a 1-in-200-year earthquake that occurs between 35 to 55 weeks into the pandemic event. Some of the assumptions for the influenza simulation are modified for the population affected by the earthquake to account for its impacts on disease transmission dynamics and public health response measures. Timing of the earthquake clash was varied randomly across the set of national scenarios to illustrate the variation in outcomes that can result from differences in timing. This would reasonably maintain the statistical relationship of the clash event occurrence and avoid presenting scenarios that are statistically far more remote than the original clash probability. Put differently, the modeling did not specifically focus on capturing the greatest impacts by selecting the occurrence time of the shock event at the worst possible point along the epicurve, unlike other work which investigates compounding impacts in the extreme tail of the probability distribution.[31]

The analysis assumes that a proportion of the population affected by the earthquake will be displaced into a shelter or other setting, resulting in increased transmission due to crowding and increased interpersonal contact. The analysis also assumes that hospital capacity will be affected, resulting in increased mortality from influenza, and that vaccine distribution will be affected.

---

[31] See for example O. Mahul, I. Monasterolo, and N. Ranger. 2021. Learning from COVID-19 and Climate Change: Managing the Financial Risks of Compound Shocks. *World Bank Blogs*. 11 June. https://blogs.worldbank.org/climatechange/learning-covid-19-and-climate-change-managing-financial-risks-compound-shocks.

For the population in modified Mercalli intensity (MMI) bands below VI, the analysis assumes that the earthquake will not result in sufficient disturbance to cause a significant increase in transmission. For the population in the MMI VI band (significant damage), a 5-day impact is assumed. For the population in the MMI bands above VI (severe to catastrophic damage), a 21-day impact is assumed. During the impact period, the reproduction number is increased to 3.5 for the affected population. Due to damage to hospitals in the impacted area, the analysis assumes the CFR is doubled over 7 days in the affected population. Due to damage to pharmacies, the analysis assumes that the rate of vaccination is decreased over 7 days in the affected population, based on the percentage of pharmacies damaged.

Flood Clash Scenario

The flood clash scenario is a combination of the influenza pandemic described above and a 1-in-200-year flood which is varied coinciding with the rainy season for the region. Some of the assumptions for the influenza simulation are modified for the population affected by the flood to account for its impacts.

The modeling assumes that (i) a proportion of the population affected by the flood will be displaced into a shelter or other setting and result in increased transmission, (ii) hospital capacity will be affected and result in increased mortality from influenza, and (iii) vaccine distribution will be affected.

For the population affected by less than 2 meters of flooding, the analysis assumes that there is not enough disturbance to cause a significant increase in transmission. For the population affected by 2–3 meters of flooding (significant damage), a 5-day impact is assumed. For the population affected by 3 or more meters of flooding (severe to catastrophic damage), a 21-day impact is assumed.

During the impact period, the reproduction number is increased to 3.5 for the affected population. Due to damage to hospitals in the impacted area, the analysis assumes the CFR is doubled over 7 days in the affected population. Due to damage to pharmacies, it is assumed that the rate of vaccination is decreased over 7 days in the affected population, based on the percentage of pharmacies damaged.

3.3 Results

Overview

The output of the simulated clash scenarios reveals that the combined effect of a disaster event such as an earthquake or flood can significantly increase the number of infections and deaths experienced from an influenza pandemic depending on the timing of the disaster event and the proportion of the population impacted. Modeled weekly new infections and deaths for the baseline scenario is shown in Figure 5. Modeled weekly new infections and deaths for the flood scenario is shown in Figure 6. The total number of infections and deaths from the three scenarios is summarized in Table 4.

The clash scenarios occur at different times in different countries and therefore the impact of the scenario is not comparable between countries. These scenarios should be interpreted as illustrative examples of the combined impact of a potential clash and not predictive of a specific outcome.

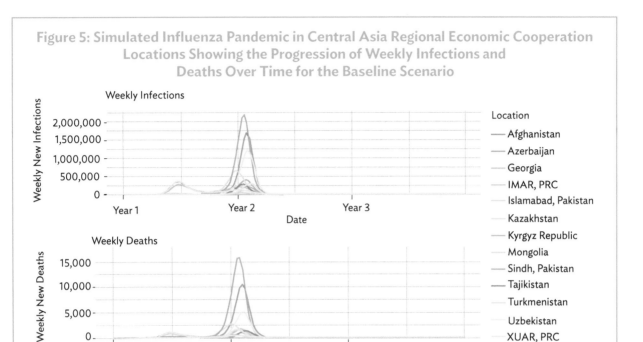

Figure 5: Simulated Influenza Pandemic in Central Asia Regional Economic Cooperation Locations Showing the Progression of Weekly Infections and Deaths Over Time for the Baseline Scenario

IMAR = Inner Mongolia Autonomous Region, PRC = People's Republic of China, XUAR = Xinjiang Uygur Autonomous Region.
Source: Consultant team modeling.

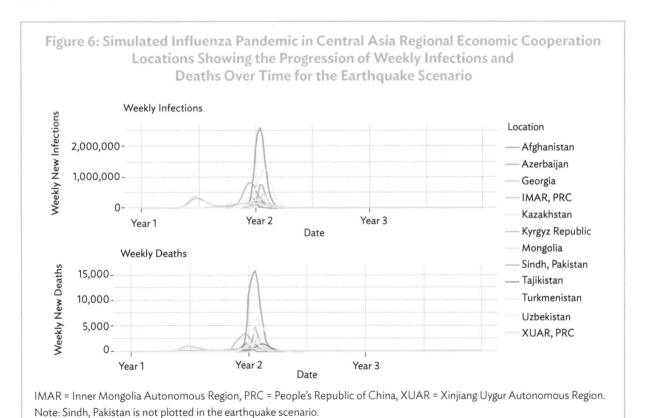

Figure 6: Simulated Influenza Pandemic in Central Asia Regional Economic Cooperation Locations Showing the Progression of Weekly Infections and Deaths Over Time for the Earthquake Scenario

IMAR = Inner Mongolia Autonomous Region, PRC = People's Republic of China, XUAR = Xinjiang Uygur Autonomous Region.
Note: Sindh, Pakistan is not plotted in the earthquake scenario.
Source: Consultant team modeling.

Figure 7: Simulated Influenza Pandemic in Central Asia Regional Economic Cooperation
Locations Showing the Progression of Weekly Infections and
Deaths Over Time for the Flood Scenario

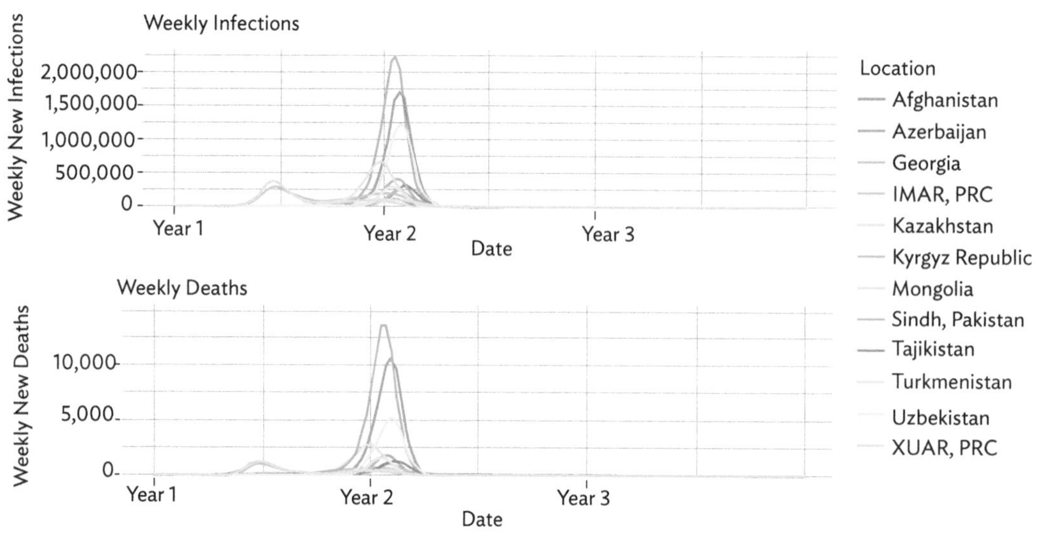

IMAR = Inner Mongolia Autonomous Region, PRC = People's Republic of China, XUAR = Xinjiang Uygur Autonomous Region.
Note: Islamabad, Pakistan is not plotted in the earthquake scenario.
Source: Consultant team modeling.

Table 4: Total Number of Infections and Deaths Attributed to Pandemic Influenza
for the Simulated Baseline and Clash Scenarios Over 3 Years

Location	Baseline		Earthquake		Flood	
	Infections	Deaths	Infections	Deaths	Infections	Deaths
Afghanistan	13,648,471	81,891	15,916,488	101,408	13,666,639	82,064
Azerbaijan	3,498,225	13,993	4,201,841	19,427	3,499,670	14,005
China, People's Republic of, Inner Mongolia Autonomous Region	6,344,536	19,034	6,370,474	19,115	NA	NA
China, People's Republic of, Xinjiang Uygur Autonomous Region	5,768,416	17,306	6,575,946	19,827	NA	NA
Georgia	1,035,110	3,105	1,114,565	3,358	1,035,714	3,108
Kyrgyz Republic	2,060,268	8,241	2,480,792	11,656	NA	NA
Kazakhstan	6,955,798	27,823	7,441,791	30,373	6,955,905	27,824
Mongolia	916,772	3,667	1,656,617	7,633	NA	NA
Pakistan, Islamabad	197,846	1,187	712,616	4,302	Not simulated	Not simulated
Pakistan, Sindh	17,962,719	125,738	Not simulated	Not simulated	NA	NA
Tajikistan	2,777,922	11,112	2,788,008	11,153	NA	NA
Turkmenistan	2,386,669	11,933	2,406,434	12,033	2,386,679	11,934
Uzbekistan	10,748,985	42,996	10,987,185	43,950	NA	NA

NA = not applicable.
Source: Consultant team modeling.

For several locations, the flood clash scenario did not result in additional infections or deaths compared to the baseline scenario. This is noted as not applicable in Table 4.

Overall the earthquake clash scenario had a significant impact on the magnitude of the influenza pandemic in most CAREC locations, causing several thousand more influenza deaths when compared to the baseline scenario. The magnitude of the uptick in infections varies across countries, as a result of the timing and severity of the earthquake or flood impact, and their level of preparedness for an outbreak. Islamabad is the location with the most significant earthquake impact; the number of infections and deaths attributed to the influenza pandemic was more than double the baseline scenario. However, in Georgia, Tajikistan, Turkmenistan, and Uzbekistan, the impact of the earthquake was less severe and there was less effect on the number of infections and deaths attributed to the influenza pandemic when compared to the baseline.

The flood clash scenario affected a much smaller portion of the population, and therefore had a smaller impact when compared to the earthquake clash scenario. It still led to excess deaths when compared to the baseline in some countries, such as in Afghanistan and Georgia, which experienced more significant flooding. As a smaller number of people are affected from flooding, the dynamics of disease spread remain (i.e., natural infections). In some earthquake scenarios, transmission is accelerated beyond the existing dynamics, resulting in a more significant impact.

One of the main drivers of the magnitude of the combined impact is the timing of the earthquake in relation to the pandemic. When the earthquake occurred during the early exponential increase in the number of infections (as opposed to occurring near or after the main peak), the impact was more severe.

The potential exacerbation of influenza spread following a severe flood is much less severe than that seen due to earthquake. This is driven by the fact that in most of the locations, significant or severe flooding only impacted a very small portion of the population, especially when compared to the earthquake scenario. Moreover, this corresponds with some of the observations from COVID-19, where tropical cyclone and flooding during the pandemic did not produce noticeable or significant increases in recorded infections or deaths.

Importance of Timing

As mentioned, the timing of the earthquake clash was randomly varied across all countries. The timing of flood events was also varied to correspond to the rainy season for the region. This helps illustrates the different dynamics that may occur due to event timing. The magnitude of the peak of infections is the point at which the healthcare infrastructure undergoes the most strain. The clash scenarios can increase the magnitude of the peak significantly, resulting in the healthcare infrastructure being more overwhelmed and having decreased ability to care for sick individuals which compounds the losses. This underlines that a significant compounding event requires two tail risk events occurring, with the natural hazard impacting at a specific time in a pandemic (i.e., the week of highest growth rate of infections).

Results per Country

Afghanistan

In the earthquake clash scenario for Afghanistan, the earthquake occurs during December of the first year of the pandemic with the epicenter in Kabul. The impact of the earthquake on the Kabul population by MMI band and healthcare facilities is displayed in Table 5. The earthquake had a significant or severe impact on more than 85% of the population and damaged over 90% of hospitals and 75% of pharmacies.

Table 5: Earthquake Impact on the Population by Modified Mercalli Intensity Band and Healthcare Facilities of Kabul, Afghanistan

MMI Band	Damage Description	Population (%)
up to III	None	0.76
IV	Light	1.97
V	Moderate	9.22
VI	Significant	42.17
VII	Severe	45.89
VIII and above	Complete	0.00

Healthcare Amenity	Damage Rate (%)
Hospital	91.67
Clinic/Doctor	75.00
Laboratory	70.00
Pharmacy	76.00

MMI = modified Mercalli intensity.
Source: Consultant team modeling.

In the flood clash scenario for Afghanistan, the flood occurs in February of the second year of the pandemic with the main impact in Kabul. The impact of the flood on the Kabul population by flooding depth is shown in Table 6. The flood had a significant or severe impact on only 1.5% of the population and damaged 9% of hospitals and 1% of pharmacies.

Table 6: Flood Impact on the Population and Healthcare Facilities of Kabul, Afghanistan

Flood Depth	Damage Description	Population (%)
No flooding	None	85.79
up to 1 m	Light	8.03
1–2 m	Moderate	4.72
2–3 m	Significant	0.86
3–4 m	Severe	0.57
4 m and above	Complete	0.03

Healthcare Amenity	Damage Rate (%)
Hospital	9.03
Clinic/Doctor	10.42
Laboratory	5.00
Pharmacy	1.00

m = meter.
Source: Consultant team modeling.

The results of the clash scenarios are displayed in Table 7 and visualized in Figure 8. The baseline simulated influenza pandemic results in over 13.5 million infections and 82,000 deaths in Afghanistan after 3 years. The peak reached over 1.5 million infections and 10,000 deaths per week.

The simulated earthquake clash scenario shows that the combined impact of these events could lead to an additional 2.2 million infections and almost 20,000 additional deaths in Afghanistan from the influenza pandemic. Additionally, the peak weekly infections increased from approximately 1.5 million to approximately 2.5 million; and the peak weekly deaths from the pandemic increased from approximately 10,000 to over 15,000.

On the other hand, the simulated flood clash scenario shows that the combined impact of these events could lead to an additional 18,000 infections and almost 200 additional deaths in Afghanistan from the influenza pandemic.

Table 7: Total Number of Infections and Deaths in Afghanistan for the Simulated Baseline and Clash Scenarios

Scenario	Description	Infections	Deaths
Baseline	Total count	13,648,471	81,891
Earthquake	Total count	15,916,488	101,408
	Difference from baseline (excess)	2,268,017	19,517
Flood	Total count	13,666,639	82,064
	Difference from baseline (excess)	18,169	173

Source: Consultant team modeling.

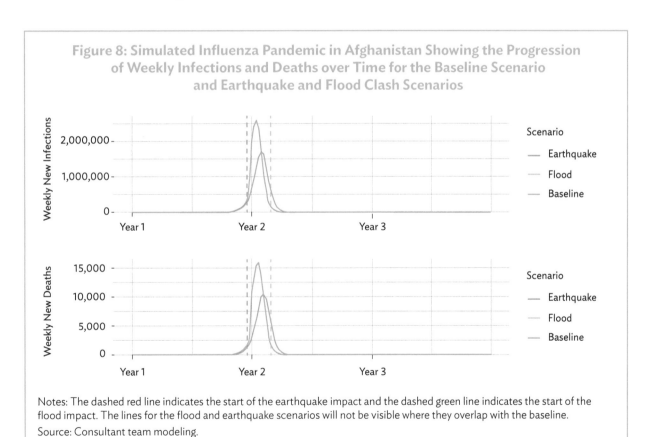

Figure 8: Simulated Influenza Pandemic in Afghanistan Showing the Progression of Weekly Infections and Deaths over Time for the Baseline Scenario and Earthquake and Flood Clash Scenarios

Notes: The dashed red line indicates the start of the earthquake impact and the dashed green line indicates the start of the flood impact. The lines for the flood and earthquake scenarios will not be visible where they overlap with the baseline.

Source: Consultant team modeling.

Azerbaijan

In the earthquake clash scenario for Azerbaijan, the earthquake occurs during January of the second year of the pandemic with the epicenter in Baku. The impact of the earthquake on the Baku population by MMI band and healthcare facilities is displayed in Table 8. The earthquake had a significant or severe impact on more than 80% of the population and damaged over 50% of hospitals and 60% of pharmacies.

Table 8: Earthquake Impact on the Population by Modified Mercalli Intensity Band and Healthcare Facilities of Baku, Azerbaijan

MMI Band	Damage Description	Population (%)
up to III	None	1.74
IV	Light	3.82
V	Moderate	11.32
VI	Significant	50.13
VII	Severe	32.98
VIII and above	Complete	0.00

Healthcare Amenity	Damage Rate (%)
Hospital	56.10
Clinic/Doctor	55.60
Laboratory	NA
Pharmacy	62.90

MMI = modified Mercalli intensity, NA = data not available.
Source: Consultant team modeling.

In the flood clash scenario for Azerbaijan, the flood occurs in December of the first year of the pandemic with the main impact in Baku. The impact of the flood on the Baku population by flooding depth is shown in Table 9. The flood had a significant or severe impact on less than 2% of the population and damaged 1% of hospitals and pharmacies.

Table 9: Flood Impact on the Population and Healthcare Facilities of Baku, Azerbaijan

Flood Depth	Damage Description	Population (%)
No flooding	None	95.71
up to 1 m	Light	4.04
1–2 m	Moderate	0.10
2–3 m	Significant	0.09
3–4 m	Severe	0.07
4 m and above	Complete	0.00

Healthcare Amenity	Damage Rate (%)
Hospital	0.88
Clinic/Doctor	1.44
Laboratory	NA
Pharmacy	1.17

m = meter, NA = data not available.
Source: Consultant team modeling.

The results of the clash scenarios are displayed in Figure 9 and Table 10. The baseline simulated influenza pandemic results in almost 3.5 million infections and 14,000 deaths in Azerbaijan after 3 years. The peak reached approximately 400,000 infections and 15,000 deaths per week.

The simulated earthquake clash scenario shows that the combined impact of these events could lead to an additional 700,000 infections and 5,000 additional deaths in Azerbaijan from the influenza pandemic. Additionally, the peak weekly infections increased from approximately 400,000 to approximately 700,000; and the peak weekly deaths from the pandemic increased from approximately 15,000 to over 4,500.

The simulated flood clash scenario shows that the combined impact of these events could lead to an additional 1,500 infections and 12 additional deaths in Azerbaijan from the influenza pandemic.

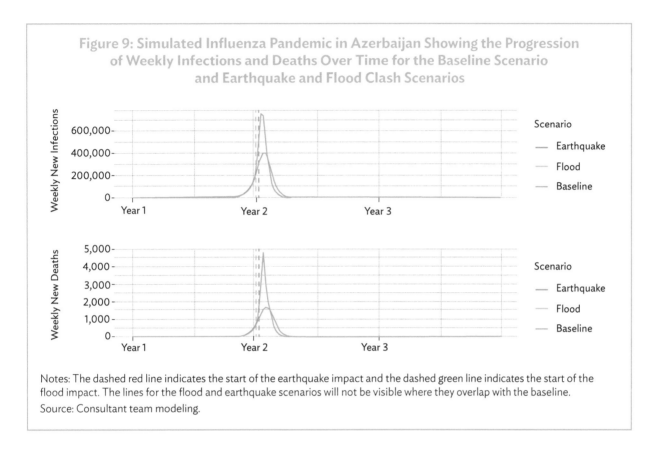

Figure 9: Simulated Influenza Pandemic in Azerbaijan Showing the Progression of Weekly Infections and Deaths Over Time for the Baseline Scenario and Earthquake and Flood Clash Scenarios

Notes: The dashed red line indicates the start of the earthquake impact and the dashed green line indicates the start of the flood impact. The lines for the flood and earthquake scenarios will not be visible where they overlap with the baseline.
Source: Consultant team modeling.

Table 10: Total Number of Infections and Deaths in Azerbaijan for the Simulated Baseline and Clash Scenarios

Scenario	Description	Infections	Deaths
Baseline	Total count	3,498,225	13,993
Earthquake	Total count	4,210,841	19,427
	Difference from baseline (excess)	712,617	5,434
Flood	Total count	3,499,670	14,005
	Difference from baseline (excess)	1,445	12

Source: Consultant team modeling.

Georgia

In the earthquake clash scenario for Georgia, the earthquake occurs during November of the first year of the pandemic with the epicenter in Tbilisi. The impact of the earthquake on the Tbilisi population by MMI band and healthcare facilities is displayed in Table 11. The earthquake had a significant or severe impact on more than 25% of the population and damaged over 50% of hospitals and pharmacies.

Table 11: Earthquake Impact on the Population by Modified Mercalli Intensity Band and Healthcare Facilities of Tbilisi, Georgia

MMI Band	Damage Description	Population (%)
up to III	None	0.00
IV	Light	0.00
V	Moderate	74.16
VI	Significant	23.94
VII	Severe	1.90
VIII and above	Complete	0.00

Healthcare Amenity	Damage Rate (%)
Hospital	50.93
Clinic/Doctor	50.83
Laboratory	50.00
Pharmacy	52.64

MMI = modified Mercalli intensity.
Source: Consultant team modeling.

In the flood clash scenario for Georgia, the flood occurs in April of the second year of the pandemic with the main impact in Tbilisi. The impact of the flood on the Tbilisi population by flooding depth is shown in Table 12. The flood had a significant, severe, or complete impact on less than 1% of the population and damaged almost 5% of hospitals and 13% of pharmacies.

Table 12: Flood Impact on the Population and Healthcare Facilities of Tbilisi, Georgia

Flood Depth	Damage Description	Population (%)
No flooding	None	85.46
up to 1 m	Light	0.94
1–2 m	Moderate	0.28
2–3 m	Significant	0.71
3–4 m	Severe	0.02
4 m and above	Complete	12.58

Healthcare Amenity	Damage Rate (%)
Hospital	4.63
Clinic/Doctor	14.58
Laboratory	0.00
Pharmacy	12.83

m = meter.
Source: Consultant team modeling.

The results of the clash scenarios are displayed in Table 13 and visualized in Figure 10. The baseline simulated influenza pandemic results in over 1,000,000 infections and 3,000 deaths in Georgia after 3 years. The peak reached over 90,000 infections and 300 deaths per week.

The simulated earthquake clash scenario shows that the combined impact of these events could lead to an additional 80,000 infections and 250 additional deaths in Georgia from the influenza pandemic.

The simulated flood clash scenario shows that the combined impact of these events had little impact and could lead to an additional 600 infections and almost 3 additional deaths in Georgia from the influenza pandemic.

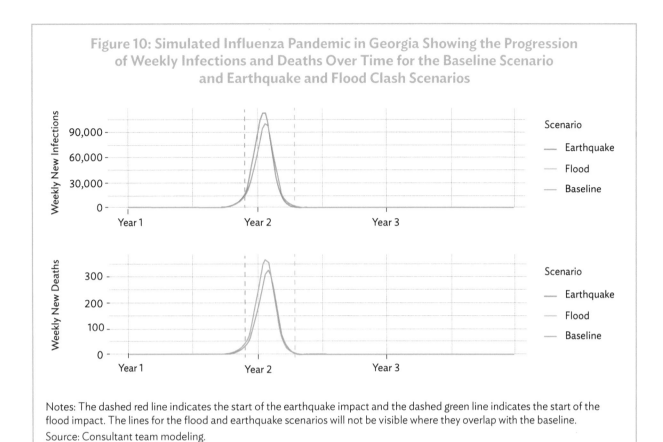

Figure 10: Simulated Influenza Pandemic in Georgia Showing the Progression of Weekly Infections and Deaths Over Time for the Baseline Scenario and Earthquake and Flood Clash Scenarios

Notes: The dashed red line indicates the start of the earthquake impact and the dashed green line indicates the start of the flood impact. The lines for the flood and earthquake scenarios will not be visible where they overlap with the baseline.

Source: Consultant team modeling.

Table 13: Total Number of Infections and Deaths in Georgia for the Simulated Baseline and Clash Scenarios

Scenario	Description	Infections	Deaths
Baseline	Total count	1,035,110	3,105
Earthquake	Total count	1,114,565	3,358
	Difference from baseline (excess)	79,455	253
Flood	Total count	1,035,714	3,108
	Difference from baseline (excess)	604	3

Source: Consultant team modeling.

Kazakhstan

In the earthquake clash scenario for Kazakhstan, the earthquake occurs during November of the first year of the pandemic with the epicenter in Almaty. The impact of the earthquake on the Almaty population by MMI band and healthcare facilities is displayed in Table 14. The earthquake had a significant or severe impact on more than 45% of the population and damaged over 40% of hospitals and pharmacies.

Table 14: Earthquake Impact on the Population by MMI Band and Healthcare Facilities of Almaty, Kazakhstan

MMI Band	Damage Description	Population (%)
up to III	None	28.43
IV	Light	10.71
V	Moderate	12.43
VI	Significant	35.95
VII	Severe	12.48
VIII and above	Complete	0.00

Healthcare Amenity	Damage Rate (%)
Hospital	40.41
Clinic/Doctor	49.23
Laboratory	NA
Pharmacy	46.12

MMI = modified Mercalli intensity, NA = data not available.
Source: Consultant team modeling.

In the flood clash scenario for Kazakhstan, the flood occurs in March of the second year of the pandemic with the main impact in Almaty. The impact of the flood on the Almaty population by flooding depth is shown in Table 15. The flood did not have a significant or severe impact on the population and damaged less than 2% of hospitals and pharmacies.

Table 15: Flood Impact on the Population and Healthcare Facilities of Almaty, Kazakhstan

Flood Depth	Damage Description	Population (%)
No flooding	None	99.57
up to 1 m	Light	0.38
1–2 m	Moderate	0.04
2–3 m	Significant	0.00
3–4 m	Severe	0.00
4 m and above	Complete	0.01

Healthcare Amenity	Damage Rate (%)
Hospital	1.71
Clinic/Doctor	0.77
Laboratory	NA
Pharmacy	1.04

NA = data not available.
Source: Consultant team modeling.

The results of the clash scenarios are displayed in Table 16 and visualized in Figure 11. The baseline simulated influenza pandemic results in almost 7 million infections and 28,000 deaths in Kazakhstan after 3 years. The peak reached over 600,000 infections and 2,500 deaths per week.

The simulated earthquake clash scenario shows that the combined impact of these events could lead to an additional 500,000 infections and 33,000 additional deaths in Kazakhstan from the influenza pandemic.

The simulated flood clash scenario shows that the combined impact of these events could lead to an additional 100 infections and 1 additional death in Kazakhstan from the influenza pandemic.

Table 16: Total Number of Infections and Deaths in Kazakhstan
for the Simulated Baseline and Clash Scenarios

Scenario	Description	Infections	Deaths
Baseline	Total count	6,955,798	27,823
Earthquake	Total count	7,441,791	33,373
	Difference from baseline (excess)	485,993	2,550
Flood	Total count	6,955,905	27,824
	Difference from baseline (excess)	108	1

Source: Consultant team modeling.

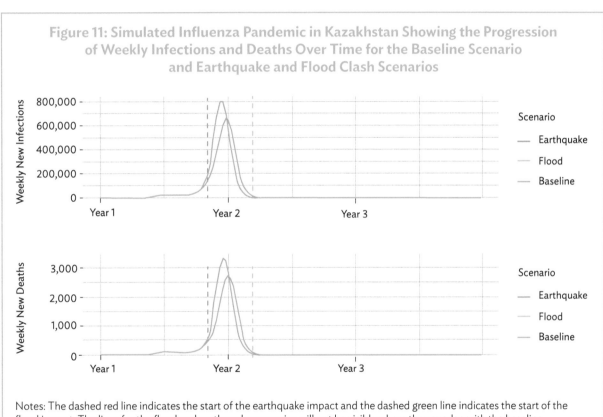

Figure 11: Simulated Influenza Pandemic in Kazakhstan Showing the Progression
of Weekly Infections and Deaths Over Time for the Baseline Scenario
and Earthquake and Flood Clash Scenarios

Notes: The dashed red line indicates the start of the earthquake impact and the dashed green line indicates the start of the flood impact. The lines for the flood and earthquake scenarios will not be visible where they overlap with the baseline.

Source: Consultant team modeling.

Kyrgyz Republic

In the earthquake clash scenario for the Kyrgyz Republic, the earthquake occurs during January of the second year of the pandemic with the epicenter in Bishkek. The impact of the earthquake on the Bishkek population by MMI band and healthcare facilities is displayed in Table 17. The earthquake had a significant or severe impact on more than 95% of the population and damaged over 85% of hospitals and pharmacies.

Table 17: Earthquake Impact on the Population by MMI Band and Healthcare Facilities of Bishkek, Kyrgyz Republic

MMI Band	Damage Description	Population (%)
up to III	None	0.00
IV	Light	0.00
V	Moderate	0.00
VI	Significant	33.96
VII	Severe	65.50
VIII and above	Complete	0.55

Healthcare Amenity	Damage Rate (%)
Hospital	87.50%
Clinic/Doctor	89.47%
Laboratory	87.50%
Pharmacy	89.17%

MMI = modified Mercalli intensity.
Source: Consultant team modeling.

In the flood clash scenario for the Kyrgyz Republic, the flood occurs in March of the second year of the pandemic with the main impact in Bishkek. The impact of the flood on the Bishkek population by flooding depth is shown in Table 18. The flood did not have a significant or severe impact on the population and damaged less than 10% of hospitals and pharmacies.

Table 18: Flood Impact on the Population and Healthcare Facilities of Bishkek, Kyrgyz Republic

Flood Depth	Damage Description	Population (%)
No flooding	None	51.64
up to 1 m	Light	45.66
1–2 m	Moderate	2.70
2–3 m	Significant	0.00
3–4 m	Severe	0.00
4 m and above	Complete	0.00

Healthcare Amenity	Damage Rate (%)
Hospital	9.09
Clinic/Doctor	10.96
Laboratory	0.00
Pharmacy	7.87

m = meter.
Source: Consultant team modeling.

The results of the clash scenarios are displayed in Table 19 and visualized in Figure 12. The baseline simulated influenza pandemic results in over 2 million infections and 11,000 deaths in the Kyrgyz Republic after 3 years. The peak reached over 200,000 infections and 1,000 deaths per week.

The simulated earthquake clash scenario shows that the combined impact of these events could lead to an additional 400,000 infections and almost 3,500 additional deaths in the Kyrgyz Republic from the influenza pandemic. Additionally, the peak weekly infections increased from approximately 200,000 to approximately 500,000; and the peak weekly deaths from the pandemic increased from approximately 1,000 to over 3,000.

The simulated flood clash scenario shows that the combined impact of these events could lead to an additional 388 infections and two additional deaths in the Kyrgyz Republic from the influenza pandemic.

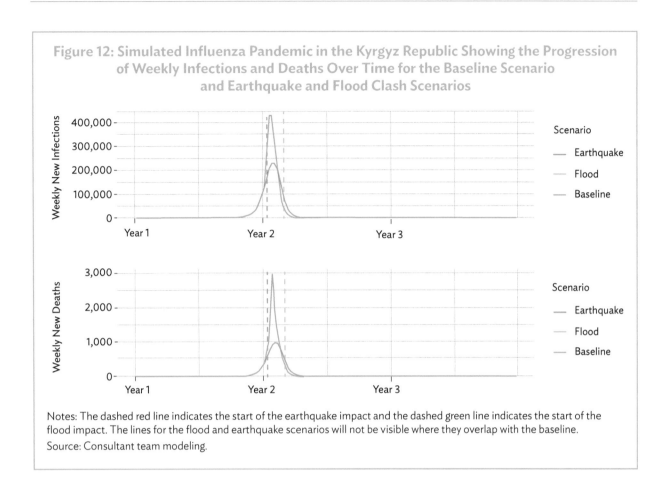

Figure 12: Simulated Influenza Pandemic in the Kyrgyz Republic Showing the Progression of Weekly Infections and Deaths Over Time for the Baseline Scenario and Earthquake and Flood Clash Scenarios

Notes: The dashed red line indicates the start of the earthquake impact and the dashed green line indicates the start of the flood impact. The lines for the flood and earthquake scenarios will not be visible where they overlap with the baseline.
Source: Consultant team modeling.

Table 19: Total Number of Infections and Deaths in the Kyrgyz Republic for the Simulated Baseline and Clash Scenarios

Scenario	Description	Infections	Deaths
Baseline	Total count	2,060,268	8,241
Earthquake	Total count	2,408,792	11,656
	Difference from baseline (excess)	420,524	3,415
Flood	Total count	2,060,656	8,243
	Difference from baseline (excess)	388	2

Source: Consultant team modeling.

Mongolia

In the earthquake clash scenario for Mongolia, the earthquake occurs during December of the first year of the pandemic with the epicenter in Ulaanbaatar. The impact of the earthquake on the Ulaanbaatar population by MMI band and healthcare facilities is displayed in Table 20. The earthquake had a significant, severe, or complete impact in almost 60% of the population and damaged over 90% of hospitals and 99% of pharmacies.

Table 20: Earthquake Impact on the Population by Modified Mercalli Intensity Band and Healthcare Facilities of Ulaanbaatar, Mongolia

MMI Band	Damage Description	Population (%)
up to III	None	1.94
IV	Light	1.95
V	Moderate	8.53
VI	Significant	24.22
VII	Severe	34.20
VIII and above	Complete	29.15

Healthcare Amenity	Damage Rate (%)
Hospital	91.00
Clinic/Doctor	86.89
Laboratory	NA
Pharmacy	99.85

MMI = modified Mercalli intensity, NA = data not available.
Source: Consultant team modeling.

In the flood clash scenario for Mongolia, the flood occurs in June of the first year of the pandemic with the main impact in Ulaanbaatar. The impact of the flood on the Ulaanbaatar population by flooding depth is shown in Table 21. The flood had a significant, severe, or complete impact on 15% of the population and damaged 20% of hospitals and pharmacies.

Table 21: Flood Impact on the Population and Healthcare Facilities of Ulaanbaatar, Mongolia

Flood Depth	Damage Description	Population (%)
No flooding	None	65.10
up to 1 m	Light	11.46
1–2 m	Moderate	5.05
2–3 m	Significant	7.40
3–4 m	Severe	6.45
4 m and above	Complete	4.53

Healthcare Amenity	Damage Rate (%)
Hospital	20.50
Clinic/Doctor	14.21
Laboratory	NA
Pharmacy	20.26

m = meter, NA = data not available.
Source: Consultant team modeling.

The results of the clash scenarios are displayed in Table 22 and visualized in Figure 13. The baseline simulated influenza pandemic results in over 900,000 infections and 3,500 deaths in Mongolia after 3 years. The peak reached approximately 50,000 infections and 200 deaths per week.

The simulated earthquake clash scenario shows that the combined impact of these events could lead to an additional 700,000 infections and almost 4,000 additional deaths in Mongolia from the influenza pandemic. Additionally, the peak weekly infections increased from approximately 50,000 to over 300,000; and the peak weekly deaths from the pandemic increased from approximately 200 to over 1,500.

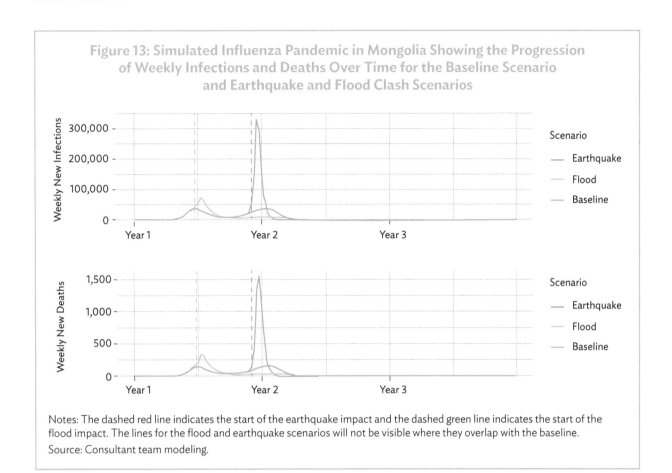

Figure 13: Simulated Influenza Pandemic in Mongolia Showing the Progression of Weekly Infections and Deaths Over Time for the Baseline Scenario and Earthquake and Flood Clash Scenarios

Notes: The dashed red line indicates the start of the earthquake impact and the dashed green line indicates the start of the flood impact. The lines for the flood and earthquake scenarios will not be visible where they overlap with the baseline.

Source: Consultant team modeling.

The simulated flood clash scenario shows that the combined impact of these events does not have a significant impact on the number of infections or deaths from pandemic influenza in Mongolia when compared to the baseline scenario. This is due to the very small portion of the population that is impacted by the flooding.

Table 22: Total Number of Infections and Deaths in Mongolia for the Simulated Baseline and Clash Scenarios

Scenario	Description	Infections	Deaths
Baseline	Total count	916,772	3,667
Earthquake	Total count	1,656,617	7,633
	Difference from baseline (excess)	739,845	3,966
Flood	Total count	NA	NA
	Difference from baseline (excess)	NA	NA

NA = There was no difference from the baseline scenario.

Source: Consultant team modeling.

Pakistan

In the earthquake clash scenario for Pakistan, the earthquake occurs during December of the first year of the pandemic with the epicenter in Islamabad. The impact of the earthquake on the Islamabad population by MMI band and healthcare facilities is displayed in Table 23. The earthquake had a significant or severe impact on more than 95% of the population and damaged over 80% of hospitals and pharmacies.

Table 23: Earthquake Impact on the Population by Modified Mercalli Intensity Band and Healthcare Facilities of Islamabad, Pakistan

MMI Band	Damage Description	Population (%)
up to III	None	0.00
IV	Light	0.00
V	Moderate	0.67
VI	Significant	33.82
VII	Severe	65.51
VIII and above	Complete	0.00

Healthcare Amenity	Damage Rate (%)
Hospital	83.52
Clinic/Doctor	80.36
Laboratory	50.00
Pharmacy	87.50

MMI = modified Mercalli intensity.
Source: Consultant team modeling.

In the flood clash scenario for Pakistan, the flood occurs in July of the second year of the pandemic with the main impact in Karachi. The impact of the flood on the Karachi population by flooding depth is shown in Table 24. The flood had a significant or severe impact on only 5% of the population and damaged 3% of hospitals and 2% of pharmacies.

Table 24: Flood Impact on the Population and Healthcare Facilities of Karachi, Pakistan

Flood Depth	Damage Description	Population (%)
No flooding	None	66.71
up to 1 m	Light	18.19
1–2 m	Moderate	8.79
2–3 m	Significant	4.04
3–4 m	Severe	1.44
4 m and above	Complete	0.83

Healthcare Amenity	Damage Rate (%)
Hospital	3.53
Clinic/Doctor	2.45
Laboratory	0.00
Pharmacy	2.30

m = meter.
Source: Consultant team modeling.

The results of the clash scenarios are displayed in Table 25, the results for earthquake scenario in Islamabad are visualized in Figure 14, and the results for the flood scenario in Sindh are visualized in Figure 15. The baseline simulated influenza pandemic results in almost 200,000 infections and 1,000 deaths in Islamabad, Pakistan (with a peak of 20,000 infections and 100 deaths), and in almost 18 mllion infections and 125,000 deaths in Sindh, Pakistan (with a peak of over 3 million infections and 15,000 deaths) after 3 years.

The simulated earthquake clash scenario shows that the combined impact of these events could lead to an additional 500,000 infections and 3,000 additional deaths in Islamabad, Pakistan from the influenza pandemic. Additionally, the peak weekly infections increased from approximately 20,000 to approximately 100,000; and the peak weekly deaths from the pandemic increased from approximately 100 to approximately 600.

The simulated flood clash scenario shows that the combined impact of these events does not have a significant impact on the number of infections or deaths from pandemic influenza in Sindh, Pakistan when compared to the baseline scenario. This is due to the very small portion of the population that is impacted by the flooding.

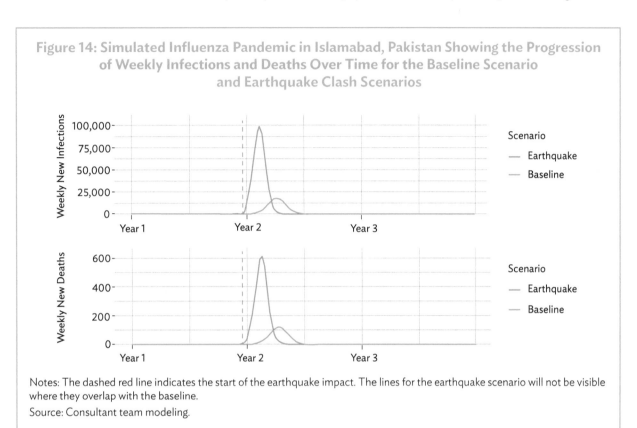

Figure 14: Simulated Influenza Pandemic in Islamabad, Pakistan Showing the Progression of Weekly Infections and Deaths Over Time for the Baseline Scenario and Earthquake Clash Scenarios

Notes: The dashed red line indicates the start of the earthquake impact. The lines for the earthquake scenario will not be visible where they overlap with the baseline.
Source: Consultant team modeling.

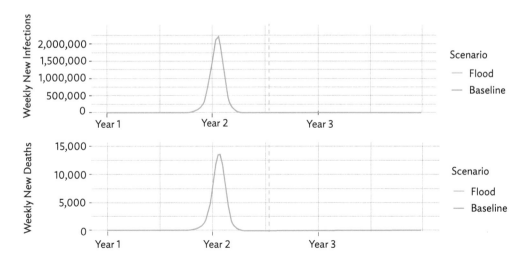

Figure 15: Simulated Influenza Pandemic in Sindh, Pakistan Showing the Progression of Weekly Infections and Deaths Over Time for the Baseline Scenario and Flood Clash Scenarios

Notes: The dashed green line indicates the start of the flood impact. The lines for the flood scenario will not be visible where they overlap with the baseline.
Source: Consultant team modeling.

Table 25: Total Number of Infections and Deaths in Islamabad and Sindh, Pakistan
for the Simulated Baseline and Clash Scenarios

Scenario	Description	Infections	Deaths
Baseline – Islamabad	Total count	197,946	1,187
Baseline – Sindh	Total count	17,962,719	125,738
Earthquake – Islamabad	Total count	712,616	4,302
	Difference from baseline (excess)	514,769	3,115
Flood – Sindh	Total count	NA	NA
	Difference from baseline (excess)	NA	NA

NA = There was no difference from the baseline scenario.
Source: Consultant team modeling.

Inner Mongolia Autonomous Region, People's Republic of China

In the earthquake clash scenario for Inner Mongolia Autonomous Region (IMAR), the earthquake occurs during October of the first year of the pandemic with the epicenter in Baotou. The impact of the earthquake on the Baotou population by MMI band and healthcare facilities is displayed in Table 26. The earthquake had a significant or severe impact in only 1% of the population and damaged over 6% of hospitals and no pharmacies.

Table 26: Earthquake Impact on the Population by Modified Mercalli Intensity Band
and Healthcare Facilities of Baotou, Inner Mongolia Autonomous Region

MMI Band	Damage Description	Population (%)
up to III	None	89.21
IV	Light	8.19
V	Moderate	1.42
VI	Significant	1.18
VII	Severe	0.00
VIII and above	Complete	0.00

Healthcare Amenity	Damage Rate (%)
Hospital	6.25
Clinic/Doctor	NA
Laboratory	NA
Pharmacy	0.00

MMI = modified Mercalli intensity, NA = data not available.
Source: Consultant team modeling.

In the flood clash scenario for IMAR, the flood occurs in July of the first year of the pandemic and mainly impacts Baotou. The impact of the flood on the Baotou population by flooding depth is shown in Table 27. The flood had a significant or severe impact on less than 1% of the population and damaged no hospitals nor pharmacies.

Table 27: Flood Impact on the Population and Healthcare Facilities of Baotou,
Inner Mongolia Autonomous Region

Flood Depth	Damage Description	Population (%)
No flooding	None	99.50
up to 1 m	Light	0.38
1–2 m	Moderate	0.11
2–3 m	Significant	0.02
3–4 m	Severe	0.00
4 m and above	Complete	0.00

Healthcare Amenity	Damage Rate (%)
Hospital	0.00
Clinic/Doctor	0.00
Laboratory	NA
Pharmacy	0.00

NA = data not available.
Source: Consultant team modeling.

The results of the clash scenarios are displayed in Table 28 and visualized in Figure 16. The baseline simulated influenza pandemic results in over 6 million infections and 19,000 deaths in IMAR after 3 years. The peak reached approximately 300,000 infections and 800 deaths per week.

The simulated earthquake clash scenario shows that the combined impact of these events could lead to an additional 25,000 infections and 81 additional deaths in IMAR from the influenza pandemic.

The simulated flood clash scenario shows that the combined impact of these events does not have a significant impact on the number of infections or deaths from pandemic influenza in IMAR when compared to the baseline scenario. This is due to the very small portion of the population impacted by the flooding.

Table 28: Total Number of Infections and Deaths in Inner Mongolia Autonomous Region for the Simulated Baseline and Clash Scenarios

Scenario	Description	Infections	Deaths
Baseline	Total count	6,344,536	19,034
Earthquake	Total count	6,370,474	19,115
	Difference from baseline (excess)	25,938	81
Flood	Total count	NA	NA
	Difference from baseline (excess)	NA	NA

NA = There was no difference from the baseline scenario.
Source: Consultant team modeling.

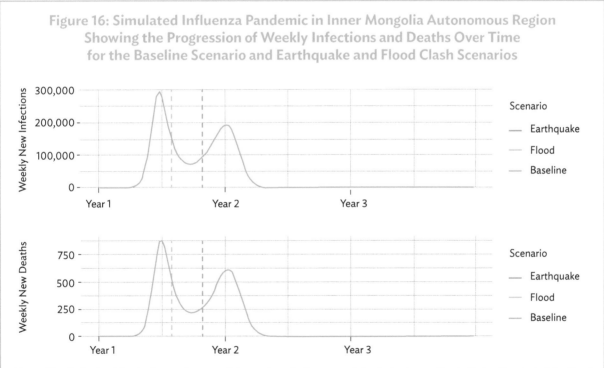

Figure 16: Simulated Influenza Pandemic in Inner Mongolia Autonomous Region Showing the Progression of Weekly Infections and Deaths Over Time for the Baseline Scenario and Earthquake and Flood Clash Scenarios

Notes: The dashed red line indicates the start of the earthquake impact and the dashed green line indicates the start of the flood impact. The lines for the flood and earthquake scenarios will not be visible where they overlap with the baseline.
Source: Consultant team modeling.

Xinjiang Uygur Autonomous Region, People's Republic of China

In the earthquake clash scenario for Xinjiang Uygur Autonomous Region (XUAR), the earthquake occurs during September of the first year of the pandemic with the epicenter in Urumqi. The impact of the earthquake on the Urumqi population by MMI band and healthcare facilities is displayed in Table 29. The earthquake had a significant or severe impact on more than 6% of the population and damaged over 19% of hospitals and 28% of pharmacies.

Table 29: Earthquake Impact on the Population by Modified Mercalli Intensity Band and Healthcare Facilities of Urumqi, Xinjiang Uygur Autonomous Region

MMI Band	Damage Description	Population (%)
up to III	None	80.61
IV	Light	1.15
V	Moderate	11.41
VI	Significant	4.88
VII	Severe	1.41
VIII and above	Complete	0.53

Healthcare Amenity	Damage Rate (%)
Hospital	19.70
Clinic/Doctor	NA
Laboratory	NA
Pharmacy	28.57

MMI = modified Mercalli intensity, NA = data not available.
Source: Consultant team modeling.

In the flood clash scenario for XUAR, the flood occurs in August of the first year of the pandemic, mainly impacting Urumqi. The impact of the flood on the Urumqi population by flooding depth is shown in Table 30. The flood did not have a significant or severe impact on the population and damaged less than 1% of hospitals.

Table 30: Flood Impact on the Population and Healthcare Facilities of Urumqi, Xinjiang Uygur Autonomous Region

Flood Depth	Damage Description	Population (%)
No flooding	None	98.35
up to 1 m	Light	1.65
1–2 m	Moderate	0.00
2–3 m	Significant	0.00
3–4 m	Severe	0.00
4 m and above	Complete	0.00

Healthcare Amenity	Damage Rate (%)
Hospital	0.76
Clinic/Doctor	NA
Laboratory	NA
Pharmacy	0.00

m = meter, NA = data not available.
Source: Consultant team modeling.

The results of the clash scenarios are displayed in Table 31 and visualized in Figure 17. The baseline simulated influenza pandemic results in over 5.5 million infections and 17,000 deaths in XUAR after 3 years. The peak reached approximately 400,000 infections and 1,000 deaths per week.

The simulated earthquake clash scenario shows that the combined impact of these events could lead to an additional 800,000 infections and 2,500 additional deaths in XUAR from the influenza pandemic.

The simulated flood clash scenario shows that the combined impact of these events does not have a significant impact on the number of infections or deaths from pandemic influenza in XUAR when compared to the baseline scenario. This is due to the very small portion of the population impacted by the flooding.

Table 31: Total Number of Infections and Deaths in Xinjiang Uygur Autonomous Region for the Simulated Baseline and Clash Scenarios

Scenario	Description	Infections	Deaths
Baseline	Total count	5,768,416	17,306
Earthquake	Total count	6,575,946	19,827
	Difference from baseline (excess)	807,530	2,521
Flood	Total count	NA	NA
	Difference from baseline (excess)	NA	NA

NA = There was no difference from the baseline scenario.

Source: Consultant team modeling.

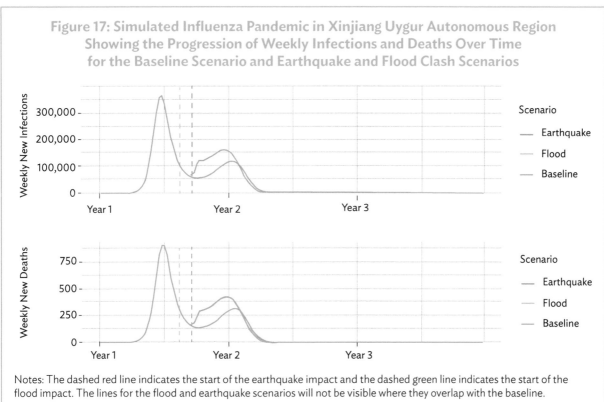

Figure 17: Simulated Influenza Pandemic in Xinjiang Uygur Autonomous Region Showing the Progression of Weekly Infections and Deaths Over Time for the Baseline Scenario and Earthquake and Flood Clash Scenarios

Notes: The dashed red line indicates the start of the earthquake impact and the dashed green line indicates the start of the flood impact. The lines for the flood and earthquake scenarios will not be visible where they overlap with the baseline.

Source: Consultant team modeling.

Tajikistan

In the earthquake clash scenario for Tajikistan, the earthquake occurs during December of the first year of the pandemic with the epicenter in Dushanbe. The impact of the earthquake on the Dushanbe population by MMI band and healthcare facilities is displayed in Table 32. The earthquake had a significant or severe impact on more than 6% of the population and damaged 50% of hospitals and pharmacies.

Table 32: Earthquake Impact on the Population by Modified Mercalli Intensity Band and Healthcare Facilities of Dushanbe, Tajikistan

MMI Band	Damage Description	Population (%)
up to III	None	0.00
IV	Light	2.84
V	Moderate	90.57
VI	Significant	6.59
VII	Severe	0.00
VIII and above	Complete	0.00

Healthcare Amenity	Damage Rate (%)
Hospital	50.00
Clinic/Doctor	47.22
Laboratory	NA
Pharmacy	49.22

MMI = modified Mercalli intensity, NA = data not available.
Source: Consultant team modeling.

In the flood clash scenario for Tajikistan, the flood occurs in December of the first year of the pandemic and mainly impacts Dushanbe. The impact of the flood on the Dushanbe population by flooding depth is shown in Table 33. The flood does not have a significant or severe impact on the population and damaged 3% of hospitals and 1% of pharmacies.

Table 33: Flood Impact on the Population and Healthcare Facilities of Dushanbe, Tajikistan

Flood Depth	Damage Description	Population (%)
No flooding	None	88.07
up to 1 m	Light	7.82
1–2 m	Moderate	4.11
2–3 m	Significant	0.00
3–4 m	Severe	0.00
4 m and above	Complete	0.00

Healthcare Amenity	Damage Rate (%)
Hospital	3.03
Clinic/Doctor	0.00
Laboratory	NA
Pharmacy	0.78

m = meter, NA = data not available.
Source: Consultant team modeling.

The results of the clash scenarios are displayed in Table 34 and visualized in Figure 18. The baseline simulated influenza pandemic results in over 2.5 million infections and 11,000 deaths in Tajikistan after 3 years. The peak reached over 300,000 infections and 1,500 deaths per week.

The simulated earthquake clash scenario shows that the combined impact of these events could lead to an additional 10,000 infections and 41 additional deaths in Tajikistan from the influenza pandemic.

The simulated flood clash scenario shows that the combined impact of these events does not have a significant impact on the number of infections or deaths from pandemic influenza in Tajikistan when compared to the baseline scenario. This is due to the very small portion of the population impacted by the flooding.

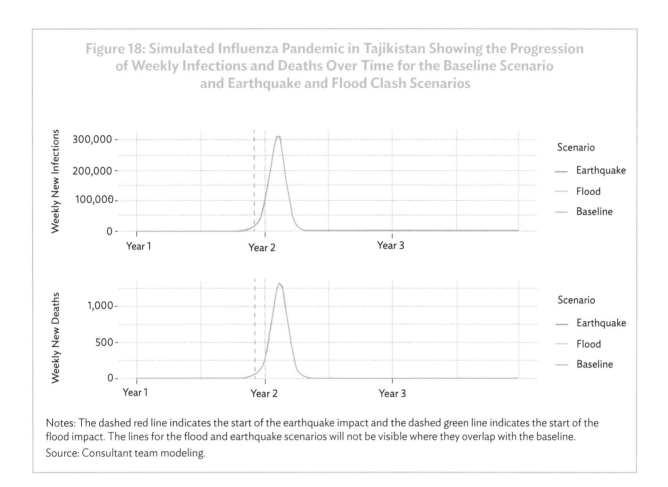

Figure 18: Simulated Influenza Pandemic in Tajikistan Showing the Progression of Weekly Infections and Deaths Over Time for the Baseline Scenario and Earthquake and Flood Clash Scenarios

Notes: The dashed red line indicates the start of the earthquake impact and the dashed green line indicates the start of the flood impact. The lines for the flood and earthquake scenarios will not be visible where they overlap with the baseline.

Source: Consultant team modeling.

Table 34: Total Number of Infections and Deaths in Tajikistan for the Simulated Baseline and Clash Scenarios

Scenario	Description	Infections	Deaths
Baseline	Total count	2,777,922	11,112
Earthquake	Total count	2,788,008	11,153
	Difference from baseline (excess)	10,087	41
Flood	Total count	NA	NA
	Difference from baseline (excess)	NA	NA

NA = There was no difference from the baseline scenario.

Source: Consultant team modeling.

Turkmenistan

In the earthquake clash scenario for Turkmenistan, the earthquake occurs during September of the first year of the pandemic with the epicenter in Ashgabat. The impact of the earthquake on the Ashgabat population by MMI band and healthcare facilities is displayed in Table 35. The earthquake had a significant or severe impact on more than 75% of the population and damaged 50% of pharmacies.

Table 35: Earthquake Impact on the Population by Modified Mercalli Intensity Band and Healthcare Facilities of Ashgabat, Turkmenistan

MMI Band	Damage Description	Population (%)
up to III	None	0.00
IV	Light	0.00
V	Moderate	26.28
VI	Significant	73.72
VII	Severe	0.00
VIII and above	Complete	0.00

Healthcare Amenity	Damage Rate (%)
Hospital	NA
Clinic/Doctor	50.00
Laboratory	NA
Pharmacy	50.00

MMI = modified Mercalli intensity, NA = data not available.

Source: Consultant team modeling.

In the flood clash scenario for Turkmenistan, the flood occurs in February of the second year of the pandemic and mainly impacts Ashgabat. The impact of the flood on the Ashgabat population by flooding depth is shown in Table 36. The flood did not have a significant or severe impact on the population and damaged less than 5% of pharmacies.

Table 36: Flood Impact on the Population and Healthcare Facilities of Ashgabat, Turkmenistan

Flood Depth	Damage Description	Population (%)
No flooding	None	75.67
up to 1 m	Light	24.33
1–2 m	Moderate	0.00
2–3 m	Significant	0.00
3–4 m	Severe	0.00
4 m and above	Complete	0.00

Healthcare Amenity	Damage Rate (%)
Hospital	NA
Clinic/Doctor	NA
Laboratory	NA
Pharmacy	4.87

m = meter, NA = data not available.

Source: Consultant team modeling.

The results of the clash scenarios are displayed in Table 37 and visualized in Figure 19. The baseline simulated influenza pandemic results in over 2.3 million infections and almost 12,000 deaths in Turkmenistan after 3 years. The peak reached over 300,000 infections and 1,500 deaths per week.

The simulated earthquake clash scenario shows that the combined impact of these events could lead to an additional 20,000 infections and almost 100 additional deaths in Turkmenistan from the influenza pandemic.

The simulated flood clash scenario shows that the combined impact of these events could lead to an additional 10 infections and 1 additional death in Turkmenistan from the influenza pandemic.

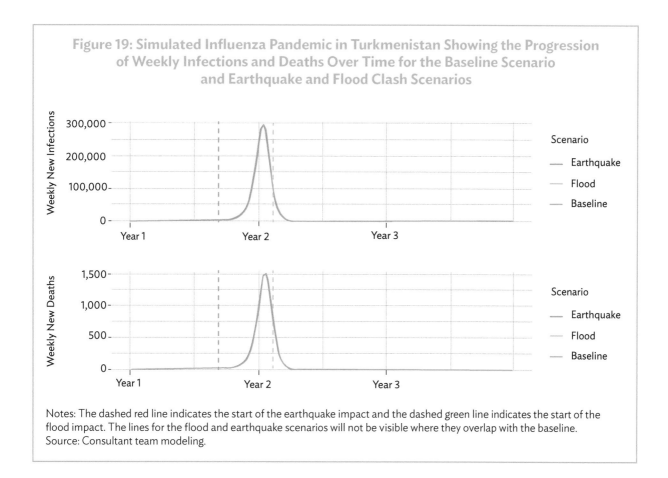

Figure 19: Simulated Influenza Pandemic in Turkmenistan Showing the Progression of Weekly Infections and Deaths Over Time for the Baseline Scenario and Earthquake and Flood Clash Scenarios

Notes: The dashed red line indicates the start of the earthquake impact and the dashed green line indicates the start of the flood impact. The lines for the flood and earthquake scenarios will not be visible where they overlap with the baseline.
Source: Consultant team modeling.

Table 37: Total Number of Infections and Deaths in Turkmenistan for the Simulated Baseline and Clash Scenarios

Scenario	Description	Infections	Deaths
Baseline	Total count	2,386,669	11,933
Earthquake	Total count	2,406,434	12,033
	Difference from baseline (excess)	19,765	99
Flood	Total count	2,386,679	11,934
	Difference from baseline (excess)	10	1

Source: Consultant team modeling.

Uzbekistan

In the earthquake clash scenario for Uzbekistan, the earthquake occurs during September of the first year of the pandemic with the epicenter in Tashkent. The impact of the earthquake on the Tashkent population by MMI band and healthcare facilities is displayed in Table 38. The earthquake had a significant or severe impact on more than 95% of the population and damaged over 50% of hospitals and pharmacies.

Table 38: Earthquake Impact on the Population by Modified Mercalli Intensity Band and Healthcare Facilities of Tashkent, Uzbekistan

MMI Band	Damage Description	Population (%)
up to III	None	0.00
IV	Light	0.00
V	Moderate	4.05
VI	Significant	91.71
VII	Severe	4.24
VIII and above	Complete	0.00%

Healthcare Amenity	Damage Rate (%)
Hospital	54.00
Clinic/Doctor	55.29
Laboratory	NA
Pharmacy	56.11

MMI = modified Mercalli intensity, NA = data not available.
Source: Consultant team modeling.

In the flood clash scenario for Uzbekistan, the flood occurs in March of the second year of the pandemic and mainly impacts Tashkent. The impact of the flood on the Tashkent population by flooding depth is shown in Table 39. The flood did not have a significant or severe impact on the population and damaged less than 1% of hospitals and pharmacies.

Table 39: Flood Impact on the Population and Healthcare Facilities of Tashkent, Uzbekistan

Flood Depth	Damage Description	Population (%)
No flooding	None	99.49
up to 1 m	Light	0.36
1–2 m	Moderate	0.09
2–3 m	Significant	0.00
3–4 m	Severe	0.00
4 m and above	Complete	0.06

Healthcare Amenity	Damage Rate (%)
Hospital	0.00
Clinic/Doctor	0.40
Laboratory	NA
Pharmacy	0.20

m = meter, NA = data not available.
Source: Consultant team modeling.

The results of the clash scenarios are displayed in Table 40 and visualized in Figure 20. The baseline simulated influenza pandemic results in over 10.5 million infections and 43,000 deaths in Uzbekistan after 3 years. The peak reached over 1.2 million infections and 5,000 deaths per week.

The simulated earthquake clash scenario shows that the combined impact of these events could lead to an additional 200,000 infections and almost 1,000 additional deaths in Uzbekistan from the influenza pandemic.

The simulated flood clash scenario shows that the combined impact of these events does not have a significant impact on the number of infections or deaths from pandemic influenza in Uzbekistan when compared to the baseline scenario. This is due to the very small portion of the population impacted by the flooding.

Table 40: Total Number of Infections and Deaths in Uzbekistan
for the Simulated Baseline and Clash Scenarios

Scenario	Description	Infections	Deaths
Baseline	Total count	10,748,985	42,996
Earthquake	Total count	10,987,185	43,950
	Difference from baseline (excess)	238,200	954
Flood	Total count	NA	NA
	Difference from baseline (excess)	NA	NA

NA = There was no difference from the baseline scenario.
Source: Consultant team modeling.

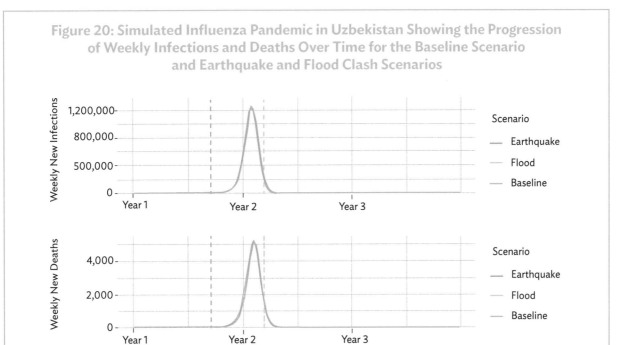

Figure 20: Simulated Influenza Pandemic in Uzbekistan Showing the Progression
of Weekly Infections and Deaths Over Time for the Baseline Scenario
and Earthquake and Flood Clash Scenarios

Notes: The dashed red line indicates the start of the earthquake impact and the dashed green line indicates the start of the flood impact. The lines for the flood and earthquake scenarios will not be visible where they overlap with the baseline.
Source: Consultant team modeling.

4 Implications and Conclusions

The potential for compound risk is present at all times, as various natural hazards may co-occur and have reinforcing and amplifying effects on population health and other outcomes. The probability of event co-occurrence and amplification is somewhat greater in the case of infectious disease epidemics and pandemics, simply due to the fact that these events occur over longer time intervals, and thus provide more opportunity for other exogenous shocks to occur. CAREC member countries have faced compound risk during the COVID-19 pandemic.

The scientific evidence available to date broadly suggests that serious epidemics are relatively unlikely to be initiated by other natural hazards. This is due in large part to recognition of the threat by public health officials, and strong actions being generally highly effective in minimizing the risk. The probability of epidemics following other natural hazard events may increase markedly in low-income and conflict-affected countries due to public health actions being less likely to be taken and/or less effective.

The scientific evidence and modeling results presented here suggest that the compounding dynamics of pandemic risk are complex, and vary by the specific natural hazard in question, its impacts on the population, and on the state of public health infrastructure. There is no clear-cut pattern to be specifically addressed across CAREC member countries. Moreover, the specific risk of a natural hazard occurring during an outbreak and significantly accentuating disease spread requires a series of circumstances to occur—most importantly coincidence in time with substantial transmission, in particular, a rapidly rising or just peaked infection wave. The empirical evidence from natural hazard shocks occurring during the COVID-19 pandemic supports this conclusion.

There is considerable uncertainty regarding the economic consequences of compounding risks. Techniques for modeling the joint effects of multiple hazards are in their relative infancy, due to data limitations and limited theoretical development to date. As such, modeling brings a high degree of uncertainty and variability around key assumptions. While the default risk modeling approach of summing losses from two coincident events is unsatisfying, more complex estimation techniques require using strong assumptions about complex interaction effects that cannot be justified and may yield misleading results. This analysis demonstrates a meaningful increase in influenza pandemic caseload and mortality due to a coincident earthquake with specific timing. It could be expected that this would result in greater economic impact, certainly in terms of the intrinsic value of lives and economic productivity lost due to elevated morbidity and early mortality, and also in terms of the negative shock to national income.

However, it is also possible to identify scenarios where social measures to control the disease spread result in reduced impacts on people and economic activity from a given natural hazard event. Likewise, flows of domestic and international spending for response and recovery to both the pandemic and the coincident natural hazard event may flow more freely due to the higher international profile of such compounding hazard events. These two examples indicate the complexity of assigning a modeled economic loss figure to a compounded event, and that any modeling of economic compounding would need to be tailored to the specific combination of natural hazards with pandemic risk (potentially also taking into account variations within pandemic risk, such as the pathogen of concern, its transmission dynamics, and economic impact).

For CAREC member countries, compound risk may pose a challenge in the form of elevated costs of response due to (i) higher operational complexity; (ii) longer timelines required to undertake reconstruction following physical damage during ongoing disease transmission; and (iii) depending on the scale, intensity, and economic disruptiveness of the pandemic, higher costs for procurement of equipment and materials resulting from supply interruptions or price shocks. These effects are thinly researched but potentially consequential, and should be borne in mind as a distinct aspect of the economic risk posed by compounding events. It is notable that catastrophe risk models do often attempt to capture such factors as demand surge, but this is generally limited to impacts on insurance claims costs and resolution timelines.

Compound risk through these mechanisms should not be ignored. It should, however, be placed in the context of the range of disaster risks faced by CAREC member countries. There is instead a need for dedicated contingency and crisis planning which focuses on the joint effects of a range of natural hazards and infectious disease risk. This should occur at the regional, country, and subnational level, considering the infectious disease risks that are salient to each geography as well as the specific natural hazards of concern.

In addition to conducting scenario planning exercises and developing operational plans for compound risk response, country risk managers and public health efforts can use the information from this study in refining their operational plans for natural hazards so as to reduce risk compounding. For example, emergency planners considering emergency housing following an earthquake could develop plans requiring larger numbers of small temporary shelters rather than mass sheltering populations that are temporarily homeless following an earthquake. Similarly, contingency planners could develop plans for decentralized food and water distribution following the occurrence of an earthquake or flood during a pandemic, to ensure that humanitarian relief is distributed without significantly increasing contact and contagion.

Furthermore, once an epidemic or pandemic has begun, existing crisis response plans for other natural hazards should be quickly reviewed, taking into account specific aspects of the infectious disease (for example, transmission mechanism, infectious period, age-specific morbidity, and mortality rates). These and other factors may determine whether and how operational plans need to be adapted to limit risk compounding and enable essential response efforts for the natural hazard. This type of refinement may, in the case of an ongoing pandemic, help limit spikes in disease transmission from population crowding. There will be opportunities to digest a large volume of scientific and operational evidence from a range of compound risk events from COVID-19, and to link public health experts with other disaster risk practitioners to develop comprehensive and country-specific guidance.

Lightning Source UK Ltd.
Milton Keynes UK
UKHW052005080622
404155UK00014B/146